What Moves You?

Every dissertation is in...vidual and unique – particularly for dance students, who must combine a wide range of ...oaches into a tailor-made research methodology.

What Moves You? fo... a creative approach to dissertations and final projects. By guiding the development of a ...nal study programme, this volume encourages dance students to take ownership of their ...istic and academic work, a skill essential both to successful undergraduate study, and to ...king the first steps towards a career in dance.

Rather than pr...po... a prescriptive, step-by-step mantra, Charlotte Nichol and Lise Uytterhoeven dra...v u... ...n contributions from students, teachers, examiners and practitioners to broaden the no...tion ... 'research' and demystify the purpose of the dissertation.

Charlotte Nichol is ...issertation Co-ordinator and Lecturer in Dance at Buckinghamshire New University, UK.

Lise Uytter... ...n is Head of Learning and Teaching, and Senior Lecturer at London Studio Centr...

What Moves You?

Shaping Your Dissertation in Dance

Charlotte Nichol and Lise Uytterhoeven

Routledge
Taylor & Francis Group

LONDON AND NEW YORK

First published 2017
by Routledge
2 Park Square, Milton Park, Abingdon, Oxon OX14 4RN

and by Routledge
711 Third Avenue, New York, NY 10017

Routledge is an imprint of the Taylor & Francis Group, an informa business

British Library Cataloguing in Publication Data

A catalogue record for this book is available from the British Library

Library of Congress Cataloguing in Publication Data
A catalog record for this book has been requested

ISBN: 978-1-138-85729-2 (hbk)
ISBN: 978-1-138-85730-8 (pbk)
ISBN: 978-1-315-71878-1 (ebk)

Typeset in Bembo
by Out of House Publishing
Printed and bound by CPI Group (UK) Ltd, Croydon, CR0 4YY

Contents

Foreword

Professor Vida L. Midgelow

School of Media and Performing Arts, Middlesex University

Dance as an academic discipline is a relative newcomer to the university. Yet, as the wealth of undergraduate courses now available in dance attest, it is now a well-established subject of study. Students in this growing field draw upon a wide range of critical perspectives and methodologies in order to illuminate dance as social, cultural and aesthetic practice. Indeed, the examples from real student projects that run through this book begin to reveal the rich breadth of topics that are being addressed by our undergraduates. Just this last academic year my own students tackled topics that included: dance with children on the autistic spectrum, a studio investigation of mindfulness in dance, contemporary dance training in the UK and a study of Africanist presence in selected choreographies by UK-based artists. These students used methodologies such as action research, ethnography, practice-based research and phenomenology, drawing on established research in dance as well as areas such as education, health and postcolonial studies, to name but a few.

Such perspectives and interdisciplinary approaches are underpinned by the skills of dance analysis and the ability to observe and critique dance practices in detail. While the concepts and skills of and for dance analysis have seemingly been less to the fore in recent years, I am pleased to see that they are referenced here. Without the ability to see, describe and articulate movement patterns in detail, research on dance can too easily become subsumed into cultural studies more broadly.

There is also a growing interest in how writing about dance can reflect the embodied experience of dancing, or indeed watching dancing. As I have suggested elsewhere, much current practice-based research attempts to write *from* rather than *only* about the bodily experience of moving. This interest is evident in the title of this new guide for undergraduates and in the useful prompts for thinking and writing that the authors offer.

This text, as a guide specifically for dance students, enables something of the particularities of the discipline to come through and this is most welcomed. The authors offer a metaphoric 'guiding hand' through the processes of selecting, shaping and writing what is, for most undergraduates, their first extended independent study. I look forward to using this guide with my students as they undertake this challenging task and as they look towards their futures.

Foreword

Professor Sherril Dodds

Boyer College of Music and Dance, Temple University

Although I did not write my undergraduate dissertation on a dance topic, I still completed a sizeable research project that culminated in a 12,000-word written study on the art film *Drowning by Numbers*. This experience showed me that I could bring a passion, in this instance the quirky and experimental cinema of director Peter Greenaway, into conversation with my academic work. It also taught me the fine balance between a heartfelt enthusiasm for watching this film over and over again, and the need to approach my research with a critical distance and a methodical framework. Several years later, I was required to deliver a final year undergraduate module, *Research Methodologies*, designed to guide and support students through the dissertation process. For this, I drew on my own experiences of dissertation and thesis writing, and the tacit knowledge I had gained from supervising student research. While I could turn to some useful sources within the dance field for particular theories and methods, or helpful generic guides that were intentionally broad in scope, I lacked a single volume that cogently addressed dissertation writing for dance students.

I am therefore incredibly grateful to the authors of *What Moves You?* for taking on this ambitious task. They offer a compelling case for 'writing' about 'dancing' and the purpose this serves for the future of the field, as well as acknowledging more recent moves to 'dance' as a way to think critically about 'dance' in the area of practice-led research. The writing and structure of the book are clear and accessible, and the authors provide plenty of examples, exercises and student reflections on the entire dissertation process, from identifying a topic to writing the conclusion. Although aimed at undergraduate dissertation writing, the book sets in place some excellent guidelines for students who go on to pursue masters or doctoral research. *What Moves You?* has certainly pushed me to address some new ideas, and it will be invaluable both for undergraduate student researchers and those teaching dissertation writing in dance.

Acknowledgements

With thanks to all our students past and present, who have helped and continue to assist us in developing effective approaches to researching dance. Thank you to colleagues and peers who have provided support and advice, and to student contributors for sharing their experience. Particular thanks goes to graduates Naomi Barber, Amy Guilliatt, Anna-Lise Marie Hearn and Emily Labhart for sharing their stories of their dissertation experience. Thank you to artist Felicity Cormack for creating the beautiful illustrations in the book, and to dancers Luke Brown, Elena Fairburn, Georgia Fletcher, Travis Sumner and Melody Tamiz for spending an inspirational morning in the studio as models for these. Also, thank you to Jacqueline Back and her dancers for the photograph on the front cover of the paperback edition.

In writing this book we have come across a wealth of existing research and resources in dance scholarship. They are testament to the richness and diversity of the field. These resources have inspired us and we believe will inspire and encourage students undertaking research projects of their own.

Introduction

This book is a guide to undergraduate research in dance and particularly supports students with their dissertation or final year project. It aims to serve as a companion to the research process and acts as a tool for navigating the dance field in all its richness and complexity.

Beyond the format of a traditional dissertation, in recent years, degree programmes have embraced a broader variety of possibilities. These include practice-based research, interdisciplinary research, lecture demonstrations, performances, extended essays and research reports. *What Moves You? Shaping Your Dissertation in Dance* supports the broad range of possibilities and approaches. Throughout this book, we recognise that as a reader you might identify yourself as student, researcher, practitioner or tutor. You may also understand your research to cut across these identities. You might have an interest in dance whilst your main focus is on another discipline. Whatever your position, this book approaches dance research as a process of identifying a focus and evolving a framework of exploration in an effort to facilitate your project.

Within the scholarship of learning and teaching in higher education, the dissertation has come under review and educators have begun to suggest enhancements that enable students to develop graduate skills for life beyond their studies. The dissertation as a key learning opportunity to undertake independent research is continually shifting and changing. Rather than thinking about the dissertation as a traditional fixed form, you are encouraged to make this learning opportunity suit your individual interests and learning needs. The university or college at which you are studying will have clear guidelines and structures in place about the requirements of your dissertation. The guidance and support offered in this study companion seek to complement and not contradict these processes that are specific to your institution. You will need to carefully negotiate your individual approach to the dissertation with the tutors at your university or college to ensure that you strike a balance between the institutional requirements and your particular interests and learning needs, creativity and innovation.

Research in dance

Research derives from the French word *rechercher* meaning 'to search for' and it is often defined in the most basic terms as a search for knowledge through the application of a structured approach that attempts to uncover this knowledge. As a process, it is an unfolding inquiry that you identify and carry out to uncover knowledge around a particular problem, question or topic. This unfolding process is not fixed, but allows for change and shifts as the research develops. It is expected that initial ideas will become more focused as you progress and that in light of the knowledge you uncover, your understanding of the inquiry may also change.

Researching dance comes with challenges in using language to articulate movement practices and experiential and tacit forms of dance knowledge. This complex issue of the forms of knowledge that exist in dance research – be that scientific, historical, political, social, tacit, kinesthetic and technical – will be expanded upon throughout the book. As such, it is important to recognise that various kinds of dance knowledge exist and not privilege one over another. Instead, these forms participate in a dance of their own, to broaden and inform the discipline as a whole. The most important task at the start of your research project is to identify an inquiry that best suits your skills and interests as a dance researcher.

The purpose of your dissertation research project will be to uncover or understand a particular area, topic or problem, in order to broaden your existing knowledge or develop a deeper understanding of a familiar topic. There can be a range of approaches to this search. The approach chosen will need to best suit your inquiry. Any inquiry can be researched in different ways, leading to the production of different kinds of knowledge. Whatever your approach, to access the kind of knowledge you are seeking, you may like to play with several approaches before deciding.

About the book

What Moves You? Shaping Your Dissertation in Dance takes you through the various aspects of the research process, from designing your project to carrying out the tasks and activities in the research. You will be encouraged to actively think about the best ways in which to make use of the support and safeguards available throughout the process. The book also guides you in presenting your research findings effectively. Finally, the book invites you to reflect on the impact of the dissertation as a learning opportunity beyond your current academic study.

Each chapter is illustrated by a metaphor that embodies a relevant aspect of the research process. These metaphors acknowledge that the different stages of the research process entail activities that require a different focus, energy and sensibility. We hope that you will find it useful to explore these metaphors and the various qualities they inspire.

Throughout the book, we encourage you to actively take ownership of the research process and make well-reasoned and effective decisions. Each chapter provides direction through focus points for reflection, practical planning activities, diagrams outlining the established and emerging ways of working in the field, and lists of resources that are at the heart of scholarship in dance. You are invited to actively write down your reflections prompted by various focus points and your responses as you complete the activities in each chapter, either following the order in which you encounter them in the book or according to what seems most appropriate for your project at the time of working. You can also earmark reflective activities for another time. There is also much value in revisiting an activity at a later date and comparing how your thoughts have developed compared to earlier stages in the project. Some activities are designed to be done with others and some can be adapted by tutors to be done in a classroom or an online setting.

We recommend that you keep a process journal while working on your dissertation, from its initial conception through to the submission of your work for assessment, and perhaps even beyond. The process journal aims to record your thoughts and reflections on the research material as your project is taking shape. It is therefore different from research notes that merely gather information and material for your dissertation, although this can, of course, happen in the same document. Record the outcomes of the reflective activities in this book in your process journal. It is likely that some of your reflections will feature in your dissertation submission in some way, perhaps reworded or repackaged.

Dance writing

The dissertation or final year project is a learning opportunity that develops and challenges your communication skills, particularly in writing but increasingly also in choreographic, visual, oral and online modes. Written communication tends to play an important role in dissertations and final year projects of any kind, whether practice-based or theoretical. Yet, writing and language are often at odds with dance experiences.

As dancers, our thinking can sometimes be caught between our embodied experience of dance as artists, spectators or researchers, and language. It can help to register and acknowledge that translating dance experiences into words is hard. Moreover, some dance scholars accept that dance writing is by definition a limited representation of dance experience or, in other words, always inadequate. So, why should we even try to write about, through or with dance?

It can help to think about dance writing as a tool to reach people who are not yet familiar with dance: participants, spectators, students, etc. Moreover, being able to articulate thoughts clearly and explicitly in words can help dance artists to access support and funding for their work. It can open doors to new contexts, networks, partnerships and opportunities. Strong dance writing skills can help dancers to participate in the economies surrounding our profession.

Having strong communication skills can also help to convince people of the importance of dance. Each dance professional can become a spokesperson or advocate for dance in the broadest sense of the term. By being vocal and persuasive, professionals can work together to keep our field vibrant and expand it in new directions.

As part of *What Moves You? Shaping Your Dissertation in Dance*, you are invited to assess the reasons for dance writing in relation to your future professional aims, and plan forward to develop the skills that you think you will need in order to achieve your professional aims. The dissertation or final year project offers an extended learning opportunity for you to push your skill sets to the maximum, not least your communication and persuasion skills.

Student comments:

'If you could give a piece of advice for other students undertaking dissertations or final projects, what would it be?'

'Pick something that you are interested in and intrigued by, so that you are motivated to find out more about it. If this can be linked to future career ideas, even better!'

'Make sure you are 100% interested in your topic. Do as much research as possible and READ lots. Stay focused and don't stress.'

'Interim submission points will help you to complete your work on time.'

'Make sure you start early, plan in advance, have as many tutorials as you can and go to all the dissertation sessions and lectures offered to you!'

Chapter 1

Designing your research project

Orienteering: Imagine you are in a new city without a map or phone. The surroundings include only a few familiar landmarks. You may feel unsettled and disorientated by being in this unfamiliar place. You will have to venture out to discover this new city, to get to know what is of interest, important and necessary in order to find your place. Exploring your surroundings will assist you in understanding more about the area. Where you start will become a grounding from which to build your own path ahead.

This chapter will be useful to you in the early stages of your research project. Your university or college may require you to submit a dissertation proposal for approval. Working with the tasks, activities and guiding questions in this chapter will help you to put together a good quality dissertation proposal. However, there is much value in continuing or perhaps revisiting the activities in this chapter beyond that initial stage to ensure that you keep up your interest in the topic, that your inquiry is connected to the field and that it is shaped effectively for your research purposes.

Finding a topic that moves you

When you begin to create a piece of dance, there is usually a starting point, even if this is difficult to locate. For many, this could be:

- a question
- music or sound
- themes or topics
- a certain image or picture
- a particular space
- poetic words
- a mathematical calculation
- a kind of movement
- a letter you received
- someone else's work.

The list in some senses is endless. Maybe you can even picture yourself attempting to find initial movement material from a starting point or imagine the methods you will use to develop it further. You may even have already formed a working structure. Perhaps you are the kind of person who likes to picture the finished product, attempting to match the finished dance piece to a specific image you had in mind. Whatever your approach, the creative process is alive and animated with questions:

- How do I put across a certain sense of something?
- How do I know when to move forward with something or if something is 'right'?

- What choices do I have?
- What material should I use?
- Why am I stuck?
- What if I disagree with someone?
- How might I develop something or know when to change direction?
- How will I know when I have finished?

In some ways, your dissertation – whether practice-based or written – is like a piece of dance you might create. It is underpinned by a process of inquiry and creativity. There are choices and decisions you will make to shape your dissertation, just like in a choreographic process. At this point in your studies, you are required to find a topic or focus that will lead you into an area where questions can arise. It can be helpful to consider the skills and processes you have already developed in a dance, choreography or improvisation context and to use these to kick start your dissertation project from an intuitive starting point.

 Focus point

Let's consider for a moment the dance process of improvisation. Imagine an improvisational score in which you begin with stillness. Notice this stillness. Then read through the following list of prompts of possible interests and, as you do so, notice what moves you. Notice how something rests with you. Notice your first thoughts or images that come to mind as you read. Are you attracted to something? Does something prompt you to consider a more specific example? Or do you lack engagement, feel disinterested or positively dislike the thought of it?

- a dance style or process such as choreography
- a role such as teacher, administrator or therapist
- an area such as fitness or community
- a business in the form of a company or dance school
- a form of identity such as gender or race
- the quality or appearance of a performance
- a medium such as photography or film or other art forms
- a single word – turn, jump, look
- an image – one seen or imagined
- a concept – stillness, silence, space.

Notice what you are drawn towards. Consider why you might be drawn towards this and take a moment to write down the things you notice. Often you can be drawn towards something you are close to in some way or even passionate about. It may simply be something you wish to know more about. Try not to decide on something simply because you already know a lot about it. Instead, seek out and embrace the challenge of a new topic area, so that you can develop your existing research skills further. With this list now consider for a moment where 'dance' as a term might sit in this area of interest, perhaps where the interest can intersect the context of dance and vice versa.

In recognising your own areas of interest, let's for a moment turn to some existing areas of dance scholarship that have been developed through former research activity in dance. Table 1.1 outlines the particular areas of dance that have been established through dance studies. Reviewing this table will be useful in contextualising your research interest and will give you a starting point for finding source material. As you read, consider the focus point above and see how each scholarship area corresponds to your research interest.

There is a growing popularity of scholarly engagement in these established scholarship areas. However, this table should not be seen as an exhaustive list. It is recognised that interdisciplinary approaches to research may bring about a merging between areas and an expansion of knowledge that might lead to newly emerging topics. The body of literature and practice in dance research is continually expanding.

Table 1.1 Existing areas of dance scholarship

Topic area	Research focus	Suggested introductory publications
Popular Dance Culture	Looking at popular forms of dance, key dance figures and practices at any given time and their contexts within society. Research can be concerned with genre, technique, social and vernacular dance forms and their development and meaning within society and culture.	Blanco Borelli, M. (ed.) (2014) *The Oxford Handbook of Dance and the Popular Screen.* Oxford: Oxford University Press.
Choreography	Looking at dance making in a range of contexts. Research can be concerned with a choreographer's role, skills and identity, process and performance. Choreography in research can also be understood to suggest an organisation of particular pathways for thinking and social practice.	Butterworth, J. and Wildschut, L. (eds.) (2009) *Contemporary Choreography: A Critical Reader.* London: Routledge.
Performance Practices	Addressing current dance practice and performance in relation to a broader understanding of arts contexts. This might include the political, cultural and social concerns that relate to particular performances and performance making. It may also lie on the borders of performance art and live arts practice.	Govan, E., Nicholson, H. and Ormington, K. (2007) *Making a Performance: Devising Histories and Contemporary Practices.* London: Routledge.
Dance History	Investigating dance practices from a historical perspective. Looking at how particular histories have been constructed or formed and how they can be critically rewritten.	Carter, A. (ed.) (2004) *Rethinking Dance History: A Reader.* London: Routledge.

Topic area	Research focus	Suggested introductory publications
Dance Scenography	Identifying scenographic practice in dance, focusing on the elements that transform the performance space and evoke a particular mood or meaning in the staging or framing of a performance.	Howard, P. (2002) *What is Scenography?* London: Routledge.
Dance on Screen	Investigating dance in screen-related contexts, such as music video, TV, cinema and film. Live dance performance where screen projection is used may be a focus.	Dodds, S. (2001) *Dance on Screen: Genres and Media from Hollywood to Experimental Art.* Basingstoke: Palgrave Macmillan.
Dance and Technology	Identifying current and former technologies and their impact on dance and the dancing body. This may include mobile technologies, programming and immersive environments that challenge ideas about dance.	Dixon, S. (2007) *Digital Performance: A History of New Media in Theater, Dance, Performance Art, and Installation.* Cambridge, MA: MIT Press.
Dance in Education	Looking at the principles and practice of teaching and learning of dance in school and other settings, such as dance schools, stage schools, community settings, conservatoires and higher education.	Pugh McCutchen, B. (2006) *Teaching Dance as Art in Education.* Champaign, IL: Human Kinetics.
Dance Science and Fitness	Investigating dance injury and rehabilitation, healthy practice and performance/training issues as well as equipment testing and development. Fitness and fitness related-contexts can involve dance practice and research will be orientated to this industry.	Quin, E., Rafferty, S. and Tomlinson, C. (2015) *Safe Dance Practice: An Applied Dance Science Perspective.* Champaign, IL: Human Kinetics.
Dance and Movement Therapy	Exploring the principles of dance/ movement practices in a therapeutic context with reference to former studies in applied therapeutic settings. This can include body/mind practice, health and wellbeing from a holistic perspective.	Payne, H. L. (2006) *Dance Movement Therapy Theory: Research and Practice.* 2nd edn, London: Routledge.
Dance Management and Administration	Exploring dance management, business and administration in a variety of settings. This could include the running of a dance organisation, company or business, policy, funding and resources.	Jasper, L. and Siddall, J. (1999) *Managing Dance: Current Issues and Future Strategies.* Horndon: Northcote House.

continued

Table 1.1 Cont.

Topic area	Research focus	Suggested introductory publications
Dance Spectatorship	Examining how dance is experienced, looking at audience interpretation and its relationship to dance making and performing.	Reynolds, D. and Reason, M. (2012) *Kinesthetic Empathy in Creative and Cultural Practices.* Bristol: Intellect. Foster, S. L. (1986) *Reading Dancing: Bodies and Subjects in Contemporary American Dance.* Berkeley, CA: University of California Press.
Dance Philosophy	Investigates particular ways of thinking about dance practices and the body and assesses the relevance of philosophical concepts for understanding dance.	Sörgel, S. (2015) *Dance and the Body in Western Theatre: 1948 to the Present.* Basingstoke: Palgrave Macmillan.

A particular topic of interest may cross over into several research areas. For example, you may find you have an interest in a popular dance craze that people are recording and putting on YouTube. This could bring together the areas of Popular Dance Culture, Dance and Technology and Dance on Screen. You could have an interest in making dance that focuses on audience participation, which may bring together Dance Spectatorship and Choreography.

Considering the question 'what moves you?', can you see where your research interest might fit in with an existing area of dance scholarship? Try speaking about this topic of interest together with possible areas of scholarship to see how they sound together and if anything else comes to mind.

The following Focus point lists a selection of research projects undertaken by students working across various areas of scholarship.

 Focus point

Former topics studied by students include:

Turns – An exploration of representation and practice in contemporary dance (Popular Dance Culture/Choreography). The student explored the representation of turns in dance and further afield including spiritual practice and ecology. She developed a piece of dance engaging in types of turn researched to address questions around the sense, quality and purpose of a turn.

A feminist inquiry into fitness advertising imagery (Dance Fitness/Dance on Screen/Dance and Technology). The student used a survey method with images and open questions to a large sample of the general public, feeding findings back into a discussion, incorporating feminist theory.

Conceptual dance, is it beautiful? (Performance Practices/Dance Spectatorship). The student identified the importance of the terms aesthetics and meaning in conceptual dance. She analysed accepted examples of conceptual dance and interpreted these with reference to relevant aspects of performance theory.

Dance practice and Down's Syndrome (Dance in Education). The student looked at the strategies/effects of dance practice on someone with Down's Syndrome. She used secondary research findings to inform her questions around the topic area. Methods employed to address these questions included participant interviewing and class observation involving performers and teachers. In consideration of ethics, she communicated through other third parties for certain responses.

Connecting to the field

So, where are you now? Well, hopefully from advice you might have received from embarking on your studies and the outline of areas in the previous section, you will have found a topic of interest. At this stage, you may not know the 'inquiry' or questions you have about that particular area. Having decided on a research interest, it is important to explore former study in your topic and attempt to locate it in in a particular field already researched. This is sometimes explained as *opening up a field of inquiry*, a phrase often used to describe the process of defining the area you are looking at and developing the questions you have about it.

Table 1.1 outlined some of the main scholarship areas in dance that comprise a range of research materials, including former research studies, practice and teaching. Connecting your research interest to an area of scholarship allows you as a researcher to make connections to a wealth of sources that will help to contextualise your interest and locate it in relation to other work that exists in the area. It will also provide you with the evidence and information to articulate and develop your interest into a viable research inquiry.

Initial steps...

One of the early influences on dance studies was the discipline of anthropology, through which the significance of dance in culture was explored. Dance anthropologists sought to immerse themselves in a particular dance culture in order to identify and classify the aspects specific to that context of dance. This brings to mind images of an explorer going into a particular unknown territory, to find out what it was to exist as part of the culture, its purpose, values, beliefs and identities. Let's draw on this image for a moment to appreciate what it might mean to identify the particular field you are exploring.

Anthropologist Savyasaachi explains:

> An inquiry has its own mode of acquiring legitimacy for itself: it defines its subject, opens the field, and shapes the manner in which the 'one engaged in inquiry' is present in the open field.

Savyasaachi 1998, p. 110

Savyasaachi suggests that the particular inquiry requires 'legitimacy' or credibility, which is important for any research project. In developing your interest, moving forward requires you to demonstrate how you might effectively and credibly conduct research that is reasonable and necessary for a particular topic area. Having a clear strategy will help to refine and focus this inquiry. The key point made by Savyasaachi is that once you have a focused inquiry or exploration, this will direct the research process and shape the type of knowledge generated.

We might use the following suggested steps to help clarify this process further:

- **defining:** articulating relevant terms, issues of importance, concepts and problems within the inquiry
- **opening:** researching the area using sources, making clear the context and background that already exists
- **shaping:** forming a research methodology, engaging with methods that best suit the inquiry and conducting the research by gathering the necessary evidence, materials, documents and/or sources to enhance, highlight and tangibly grapple with the questions of inquiry
- **being present:** finding your critical, analytical, reflective and political voice in this inquiry through the research process and knowing how this sits with other voices, in order to understand the impact and importance of the research.

These interconnected processes can assist us firstly to 'define' the area of interest and 'open' up an understanding of that area. This will assist you in developing a focused inquiry. 'Shaping' can be arriving at the way in which you might carry out the research, deciding on a particular methodology, set of methods, data forms, analytical, critical and theoretical approaches. 'Being present' can involve looking at who is saying what and what is the balance of voices you have incorporated into your research and why. Voices can mean any contributor you include e.g. authors, participants, theorists or specialists in the area, practitioners, groups and organisations. From there, you can determine where you are speaking your voice amongst the rest.

These steps of defining, opening, shaping and being present might be conducted as steps in the research process. They can also be considered as overlapping and simultaneous. For example, you could think creatively about how you 'shape your voice in order to be present', 'open up a definition to broaden understanding' or 'define your process of shaping something'.

Connecting to a particular area of interest in order to identify your field requires initial research. This research should eventually allow you to create a proposal. If it is carried out in depth, it could assist in providing a detailed context of your field, towards the formation of a literature or field review.

In the next section, we will introduce strategies for framing your field of inquiry and for locating useful sources. Initial searches may leave you feeling overwhelmed. At this stage, the tendency is to have quite a broad focus that you will eventually narrow down onto the key issues or concerns that are important to your study. This is all part of the process of refining that you will go through.

Strategies for locating relevant sources

The following activities are useful for finding key material for your topic area, in order for you to begin to develop your research questions. It is important to make sure you record your search information as you go along in your process journal, so that you can reflect on your progress. When you find a relevant source, always start by recording its details (author, date, page etc. or any relevant referencing details). You may also find in making notes that diagrams, such as spider diagrams or maps, are useful visual prompts.

- Find words you associate with your topic and look at the way in which dancers, choreographers, theorists, scholars and other people of note define them. You might find that this is not easy, as they may not be using the same language. If so, are they saying similar things in a different way or do they hold opposing views to you and other key voices in the field?
- Explore a term by reading around the term itself e.g. choreography. In reading about choreography, you may find other words are discussed, such as composition, space, creative process, score and improvisation. You can then go back to the previous search with these terms or continue to read around this new set of terms.
- Having generated a broad selection of informative material, identify that which is most necessary and relevant to your inquiry or topic. This can be difficult, but is crucial for focusing and refining your research project. You should ask yourself:
  - What existing information might help in building an argument or hypothesis?
  - What material might best illustrate a point?
  - Whose perspective might support a particular concern?
  - Are there any corresponding ideas from other areas that might apply to your interest and could become a parallel?
  - What is missing from this existing information?
  - What leaves you with questions?

 Focus point

Search example:

In reading through the list, I found I was drawn towards the role of teacher, but also interested in improvisation. I remember that, when we audition, sometimes we are asked to improvise or taught material to do a structured improvisation. I wondered how you might teach improvisation or improve your ability to improvise.

Looking at the list of scholarly areas, I noticed that it fitted in mostly with Choreography and Dance in Education, because I was interested also in how people learn to improvise. So, considering this, I notice that my focus is more on improvisation now, but I am still interested in how this can be taught. What is improvisation? How have I learnt to improvise? Who teaches improvisation?

As I am not really sure yet about the kinds of words that I might need, I will explore terms by reading around improvisation and dance teaching and learning to see how other practitioners talk about it. Reading around these topics, I have found a few practitioners who use improvisation in choreographing work and some who have written about ways to improvise. I will start noting down important things they have to say or words they have used. These words might form a selection of key terms. I was interested to find that Judson Church was important for the development of improvisation, but this left me with questions about different styles of dance, particularly jazz, and if improvisation meant the same thing with different styles of dance. Once I have enough information, I will start sorting this information into sections or subtopics to my main topic.

Shaping your inquiry

This final section helps you to bring together ideas and findings into a more formal framework or proposal for study, shaping a structure with which to go forward. The guidance should be interpreted so that it aligns itself to the requirements of the particular programme of study at your institution. This section outlines general aspects of a research framework: project scope, working title, research questions, aims and objectives, and considering methods.

Where are you now? You should have identified a topic of interest, located the topic within an existing area(s) of scholarship which will, in turn, lead you to appropriate sources to contextualise your inquiry. It is now important to bring these initial ideas and research together to form a structure or framework for your research project that might enable you to clarify the direction of your study.

For example, you might explore the history and context of the area. As part of this research, you would look to identify work, processes, former research or studies and defining terms or ideas in respect of this area of interest. You could look at a specific era, style, practice, practitioners and performance work. There may be links to a particular cultural, historical or political setting or set of events. You might begin to speculate about potential links between the development of the dance or performance practice you are investigating and particular aspects of its historical, cultural or political context.

The following activity helps you to clarify the important aspects of your topic of interest, towards the development and writing of specific sections of your research project. It has been adapted from an exercise by R. Kumar (2014, p.72).

Activity: Shaping your research topic

Using the following headings, organise the information gathered so far, in order to develop a framework for your research.

1. **Identify field/subject area of interest**
    Just put a few words here to name it.
    Example: Teaching dance (scholarship area: Dance in Education)

2. **Refine**
    What are the smaller areas or subtopics within this interest?
    Examples:
    - learning strategies
    - teaching methods

- assessing dance practice
- evaluating, feedback

3. **Select**

Choose the most interesting subtopic.

Example: Communicating feedback in dance teaching

4. **Question**

What do you want to know about the area or subtopic?

Examples:

- What kinds of feedback are there?
- How is feedback commonly communicated in dance teaching?
- What is the most effective way to communicate feedback?
- How can you measure how effective it is?

5. **Direct**

Restate Step 3: Select as a main aim and then create specific objectives from questions in Step 4: Question.

Example:

Aim: To explore the role of communication in delivering feedback in dance teaching.

Objectives:

- Identify various forms of feedback and communication methods.
- Identify various modes of feedback commonly used.
- Develop a method to evaluate feedback communication based on purpose and aims of feedback.
- Test out method using specific forms of feedback communication.

6. **Assess**

How might you develop a way of meeting your objectives? What is feasible? Whose cooperation will you need?

Example: Consider the context/learning environment that you are interested in – college, school or university.

- Who will this involve – students, teachers?
- Will you have access to sufficient research participants?
- Will you get permission to observe classes?

Project scope

The project scope should describe/outline what the research will entail and, in brief, the context that is applicable or specific to that research:

- identified field/subject area of interest
- associated subtopics
- secondary contextual research
- rationale
- outcomes.

It can be difficult to identify the scope of the project when it crosses over into numerous areas of scholarship. This is why the activity above allows you to go through a process of refinement to see what it is that you are really interested in. You should keep picking away at what you will include, until you are sure it is most relevant to your research. Ask yourself constantly:

- Is this really necessary for my research context?
- Is this what I need to know in order to conduct this research?

Working out what you will include in your research is a continual process of refinement and often requires evaluation in relation to the requirements set by your institution. Often your search for a topic will either be too broad or too focused. As we can see from the previous example, teaching dance is identified as the initial interest and can be seen to align to the scholarship area of Dance in Education. Finding your focus will involve looking into this scholarship area of Dance in Education, using resources that come up under search terms (e.g. feedback in dance, embodied feedback, peer and augmented feedback, dance corrections).

Some smaller areas or subtopics may not be clearly stated by others, but you may consider them important to your research area. In the example, the learning environment might be of key interest in the effectiveness of feedback in dance teaching, but it has not really been identified significantly in the secondary research. You can therefore identify this as an area for exploration, as it appears under-researched.

 Focus points

Example of a research project scope, expanding the topic in the previous activity:

The scope of this project is to research the way feedback is communicated in dance teaching [identified field/subject area of interest].

In the area of Dance in Education, dance teaching requires continual delivery of feedback to the dance student through peer, self and teacher response [associated subtopics].

The focus of this project is to research the effectiveness of communication methods in delivering dance feedback. Research in this area concerns generally observed and suggested approaches already identified (Kassing and Jay 2003; Jones and Ryan 2015) [secondary contextual research].

This study addresses teacher feedback specifically in a Further Education (FE) environment where, through observation, methods of feedback will be identified and evaluated [focused context].

In FE, pivotal development towards future career and study opportunities becomes a focus for the student. This can be influenced by a student's learning and as such feedback surrounding this becomes an invaluable tool for dance training [rationale and outcome].

The example above is brief and can become more defined in your own research. When done as a comprehensive section of writing, this can be developed into an introduction to the research project in identifying the parameters of your research. For this, it is also important to identify what the limits of the research are and the area to which it aims to contribute. For guidance on introductions, see Chapter 4.

Working title

Developing a working title can be difficult as it is necessary to be concise and grab the reader's attention. Most importantly, it should be brief and not stray from the research subject. The following suggestions are there to assist you to form your working title, but the final title might not be pinned down until the end of your study.

- **Statement:** From the previous activity, you could just take the example in the Step 3: Select, **'Communicating feedback in dance teaching'**, and simply make this your working title. However, it is short and doesn't really draw the reader in yet. It needs further detail.
- **Question:** As you articulate your interest further, the language you will use helps to define your focus. For example in the above activity, a focus is identified on effectiveness. You might pose a question as a title, such as **'What is effective feedback in dance teaching?'**
- **Secondary research-informed:** You will have done some research and found that Jones and Ryan (2015) suggest that feedback should be aligned to the principle of dancer as 'reflective practitioner'. Your title could be **'Effective feedback and its links to reflective practice'**.
- **Method-informed:** Another form of title might be to say something about the methods used in the research project, such as **'A comparative study of feedback methods and their effectiveness in dance practice'**, suggesting that comparison is the method used to debate the effectiveness of certain feedback approaches.
- **Argument-informed:** It could be that you will be attempting to discuss a particular argument or hypothesis: **'The limitations of augmented feedback in dance teaching'**.
- **Provocative:** You may get inventive and add a touch of humour or provocation to your title: **'Feed me, teacher! Facilitating autonomy and independent learning in dance'**.

These suggestions are some of the key approaches to creating a title and you can add your own variations to these.

Research questions

Every research project is driven by a research question. When articulating the research questions in your proposal, you must be specific about the knowledge you are looking to uncover. Articulating or phrasing these can be difficult, particularly if your initial topic and starting point are quite broad. In this section, you will find useful guidance for developing productive research questions.

Time should be taken to address what questions are appropriate for the kind of knowledge you are seeking. For instance, in the example explored in the activities above, the inquiry is into how feedback can be communicated effectively. So consider for a moment you are explaining this to someone who knows nothing about your project. Firstly, you would need to explain what kind of feedback in dance you are researching, so a question could be:

- 'What modes of communication are used in delivering feedback in dance teaching?'

You would then need to detail what you mean by effective or how that might be measured. Within research, adjectives such as effective require qualification and should be measurable in terms of developing evidence for your own research knowledge. A question may be:

- 'How can we know whether communication in dance teaching is working effectively?' or
- 'How can effectiveness be measured in delivering feedback in dance teaching?'

As you can see, altering the approach to a question can alter the focus of the question as the first one addresses modes of communication and the second and third address the effectiveness more specifically. There are various strategies for formulating questions and these often involve playing with how a question sounds to make sure it best describes your inquiry.

The more information you have, the more you realise where the questions are in the topic area.

- What remains unanswered or unexplored?
- What would you like to know more about?

Perhaps you know a lot about a topic, but you feel there might be a different way of coming to know the same topic that would provide a different form of research. For example, you might move from a written inquiry to a studio-based one:

- 'In which ways do postmodern choreographers revisit the notion of narrative in their work?'

Shifted to:

- 'What are the ways in which movement can convey narrative meaning in dance performance?'

Try to avoid judgment or opinion-based questions that make assumptions without evidence. It is important to form questions that are feasible to approach using the resources and time that you have. A question such as:

- 'Why does dance cause eating disorders?'

makes great assumptions about the relationships between dance and eating disorders, and is best avoided. Instead, inquiries into dancers and body image might lead to questions, such as:

- 'How do distortions in body image affect dancers in training?'

This will, of course, shift the line of inquiry, but this adjustment may be necessary in order to find a topic that is feasible to study.

Research questions can arise from different research activities, such as literature or field reviews, studio practice and everyday lived experience. Studio inquiries can be good examples of how a practice-based research question might be formed. For example:

- 'How might movement dynamics communicate expression in dance performance?'

Once you have a question/or questions, talk this through with your tutor as this can help in developing or refining these questions.

Aims and objectives

Research proposals and introductions commonly detail the aims and objectives surrounding the project and these can be confusing terms. An aim is the proposed outcome of what you are doing and an objective is a task you will fulfil to accomplish your aim. The activity for shaping your inquiry on pages 14 and 15 helpfully provides a strategy for considering aims and objectives using Steps 3, 4 and 5.

Rephrasing your selected topic of interest using verbs, such as explore, investigate, identify, test or interrogate, can detail the nature of your research. The selected verb will make your inquiry more specific than just the term 'research' alone. In identifying your aim, check back by reading it out loud to see if it sounds like the approach you are taking. The objectives are then directly related to the research questions you have identified and are expressed like a 'to do' list. Again, pay attention to the way you articulate these and check back by assessing if these objectives can plausibly be achieved or require adjustment to make them more appropriate to the topic of inquiry. Usually you will end up with a main aim and around three to five objectives depending on how specific you are.

 Focus point

Example:

Research question: 'What are the ways in which movement can convey narrative meaning in dance performance?'

Aim: To explore ways in which movement can convey narrative meaning in the creation of a dance performance.

Objectives:

- Conduct a contextual review of choreographers' work with narrative in the field.
- Articulate through practice effective ways to convey narrative.
- Demonstrate narrative through a dance performance.
- Document insights from the creative process surrounding narrative development.

Considering methods

In the final part of the Activity: Shaping your research topic, you are asked to assess or consider the methods you will use to carry out your objectives. Part of this is to address what resources you have that are necessary to carry out your research. It can be helpful to look at the:

- when?
- where?
- what?
- who?

of your research. In the example from the activity, the learning setting is a Further Education college and the desired research participants are dance teachers and students. It could be that, in discussion with your tutor, you could find relevant organisations, places and contacts that may assist with or participate in your research. You may need to work on studio practice and so studio space may be required. You may need to use equipment in your research, such as recording devices like cameras and sound recorders, and you may need other materials if you are crossing over into other art forms.

It is also important to consider the questions and objectives you have and how you will go about using particular methods to research. In the previous activity, methods considered in the research on communicating feedback include interviews and surveys with participants. This is because the voices of teachers and students are important to this research. It may also be that teachers allow their classes to be observed, in order for the researcher to identify modes of communicating feedback as it happens. In Chapter 2, we will explore how to conduct an interview and the need to consider research ethics in working with participants. In Chapter 3, we will be looking more closely at what is meant by methodology and the various methods available to the student in approaching particular areas of research. We will be looking at the role of theory in building an argument or discussion and how different topic areas can be approached in different ways to provide new insights and perspectives.

Activity: Speaking and listening – peer exercise

In a pair, choose which one of you will be speaking first.

Facing each other, the speaker tells the listener about their research idea, including the topic, any key questions and any ideas about methods that they might use to get research data. During this, the listener must remain silent and actively listen, remembering as much as they can about what the speaker has said. The speaker concludes when conversation is exhausted and by saying that they have finished.

In the second part of the exercise, listener and speaker swap roles. This time the person who previously listened should recount to the former speaker what they heard and understood about the research idea . First, they should attempt to reflect back what they have heard and then they can add questions they have about the idea and their responses to it. During this, the listener or former speaker must remain silent, actively listening, noticing what words are used and what has been understood about the idea by the speaker.

The third part of the exercise allows the pair to have an informal discussion about the things that arose out of the exercise. The first speaker should consider if their idea was understood in the way they were trying to put it across.

- Were other words or language used to explain it that you hadn't considered?
- Was your idea misunderstood, needing further explanation?
- What questions arose about the idea?
- What responses to the idea did you get?

Care should be taken not to talk in the transition between swapping roles and only allow two-way communication in the latter part of the exercise, where there is opportunity for informal conversation. When you have completed this – swap over.

It may be advisable to give a set time limit to each section of the exercise.

Activity: Annotating a bibliographic

The example below outlines a valuable approach to annotating a research source. This means that you explain why the source is helpful to your research. Have a go at annotating your own identified material, which could be any type of source, i.e. performance, film, report, book, journal etc. Identify the numbered points for the source that are applicable. Please note that the example below is not a real source, but one made up for the purpose of this activity.

Table 1.2 Example annotated bibliographic source (fictional)

	Key
(1) Smith, C.O., Baker, B. and Howard, S.O., 2020, 'Choreography and Improvisation are the same thing', *Journal of Dance*, vol. 12, no. 2, pp. 25–43.	**(1)** Citation of resource – see citethemrightonline.com for bibliographic reference layout.
(2) In this article Smith et al. review definitions of choreography and improvisation in relation to different practitioner approaches, in order to challenge misconceptions and propose a new understanding of relationships between the two.	**(2)** Introduction – what the literature is about.

(3) The authors use analysis and interviews in the detailing of practitioner approaches and discuss findings to support proposed conclusions, weaving in the relevant theory.

(3) Aims and research methods – if applicable, what are the aims and methods used?

(4) Their research focuses on a small group of independent dance makers, who all use improvisation in making performance work. Its focus is on practice and philosophy.

(4) Scope – what areas does it cover?

(5) The article is useful to my research topic, because it introduces me to practitioners and theoretical perspectives on my topic.

(5) Usefulness (to your research/ to a particular topic). How will it be useful?

(6) The main limitation of the article is that the practitioners were restricted to one style of dance and it was a small group of practitioners.

(6) Limitations – what it doesn't offer or cover.

(7) The authors suggest that particular understandings of both choreography and improvisation were unhelpful in setting up a hierarchy of practices and proposed a new 'fluidity' in which terms became different perspectives of the same practice.

(7) Arguments or conclusions? What does it suggest or argue, or how does it conclude?

(8) This article will be useful as a starting point to investigate possible questions I have around the relationship between improvisation and choreography.

(8) Reflection (explain how this work illuminates your topic or how it will fit in with your research). When and where will you use this in your research?

This activity will help you to determine how your sources will be useful to your inquiry and to develop a critical engagement with the material by writing an annotated bibliography. Find a dance source of your own, be that a book, article, report, performance, film or web source, and provide details as in the example shown in Table 1.2.

This exercise was adapted from the University of New South Wales version.

Student comments:

'How did you start?'

'I contacted the university at which I wanted to complete my postgraduate course. I wanted to move more into Sports Physiology, something not covered very much on the undergraduate Dance Performance course that I had taken, and so my new university suggested that I do my dissertation on something that is physiology based, as this would help me with reading and research for the following year.'

'I have always been interested in dance and film and I thought this would give me the chance to explore it further in my dissertation. My project developed quite a lot from when I started researching. From a broad inquiry, I narrowed it down to screen dance, as that was the area I was most interested in.'

'To decide on my dissertation topic, I wrote a list of the areas I was most interested in within the dance field. I then did some basic research on all these topics to see where the most research and information was. Then, from this I chose two subjects I could possibly look into for my dissertation.'

Summary points:

It is important to find a topic for your dissertation or final year project that really 'moves' you, in other words that you are strongly motivated to explore over an extended period of time.

Reviewing the table outlining the 'Existing areas of dance scholarship' might prompt ideas for research topics.

In the initial stages of your research, it is vitally important to connect to the field. This means identifying the key features of the work of other research-ers in your part of the field and locating your own interest in relation to existing work.

Shaping your inquiry, or creating a research framework, involves narrowing down your project scope, formulating a working title and research questions, articulating your aims and objectives, and considering research methods.

Chapter 2

Anchor points in your learning process

Rock climbers often use anchors to prevent themselves from falling and to advance in their climb. They find or create objects, such as bolts, to which they can attach themselves temporarily in order to minimise the distance they would drop in case they do fall or in order to hoist themselves up further. You might think about anchors as consolidating the climber's progress along the way.

When tackling a new and unfamiliar challenge such as a dissertation, it is a good idea to identify the metaphorical anchor points or support mechanisms that are in place to help you along the way. What assistance and guidance does your university or college offer for the dissertation? You may be allocated a tutor who will support your progress. It may be possible to submit a draft of your text in advance to get feedback from the tutor, or – in the case of practice-based work – to show your tutor work-in-progress. There may be opportunities to share your research ideas with your peers and get support and feedback from them. There may be other specific support services in place to which you can turn. It will be key to identify what support is in place and what you need to do to access it. This includes carefully planning your time, so that you do not miss out on opportunities to receive the help on offer.

Self-managing the dissertation process

Setting your own deadlines

Setting interim deadlines for yourself is always a good idea. It involves breaking up the mammoth dissertation task into smaller activities and achievable targets, for example:

- reading a particular chapter or article
- analysing a video recording of a dance production

- writing a specific section of a chapter
- editing a chapter for grammar and writing style
- addressing feedback comments from your tutor.

It is useful to work backwards from the final dissertation submission date. Allow for a one-week buffer for proofreading and binding your dissertation. Work within the guidelines given to you by your university or college: it is likely that tutors are not available to give feedback on draft work at the last minute or over the holiday periods, so factor this into your timeline.

Sticking to your own deadlines is easier said than done. There will be hurdles for you to overcome along the way; no dissertation project ever goes entirely smoothly. Accept that this is a normal part of the process, keep a careful eye on your progress and adjust your timeline and deadlines as needed, so as not to fall behind too much.

Keeping your research focused

During the research process, you might get distracted by tangential avenues of thought and deviate too far from your initial research idea or question. Sometimes it can be hard to tell the difference between letting the research take shape and transform intuitively, and getting distracted and deviating from what the research actually is. The only person who can tell what is going on is you, which is why it is important to monitor your progress carefully and reflect constructively on how you are dealing with these challenges.

Sometimes you will need to make bold decisions about how to move forward, one way or another. A risk of not making important decisions about your research is that you may get stuck, feel paralysed and not make any progress. As long as you think the decisions through methodically and weigh up the downsides and benefits of the various options, you should have confidence in your ability to make the right decisions for your research.

It can be a good idea to keep a process journal, in which you articulate and document your thoughts about how the research is taking shape. Particularly when undertaking practice-based research, it is advisable to log your process and reflect on it in writing, so that you have a record of the different steps involved in your exploration.

 Focus point

Below is an extract from a former student's process journal:

The aim of my practice-based research is to explore the female body as a starting point for choreographic movement and to make visible certain bodily processes that are often hidden and considered 'disgusting'. I recently presented an excerpt of work-in-progress to my tutors and peers during a Scratch Night. In the discussion that followed, it became clear that some members of the audience struggled to recognise the themes of my project, let alone feel connected to them. This may be due to the divide between the work and the audience in a proscenium theatrical setting, in which spectators felt detached. It has made me think that I will need to find ways in which I can physically involve the audience in their experience of my work through stimulating the senses.

Possible ways in which this may be achieved are:

- creating an extreme aural landscape of squelching and trickling sounds
- projecting video images of extreme close-ups of the body
- abandoning the proscenium set-up so that the spectators can walk around the performance like in an art gallery
- letting the audience chew bubble gum during the performance.

Next, I will explore these possibilities in my rehearsals and at future Scratch Nights. One of the risks may be that these other strategies begin to overshadow the dance movements. I will be looking for a way in which choreographed movement, sound and image can integrate with each other, rather than drown each other out.

Dissertation support

Tutorials

Your university or college may offer the possibility to have meetings with a tutor about your dissertation progress. It is important to understand that these tutorials are intended to be led by you, the student. The tutor will not be giving you the answers to your research questions or make decisions for you in terms of what you should do. Rather, the tutor will act as a kind of sounding board, an experienced researcher who understands the challenges and can help you to think through the decisions you are faced with.

When conducting an extended, independent research project, in which you are to a certain extent becoming an expert on the topic you are studying, you and the tutor are increasingly moving towards becoming peers in a community of researchers. While tutors possess a wealth of knowledge on their subject, there are of course limits to areas on which they have expert knowledge. As a result, tutors often enjoy working with students on dissertations, because it offers them an opportunity to learn new things and expand their knowledge. So, while it is unreasonable to expect a tutor to have all the answers, it is better to begin to think of the tutor as an experienced peer with whom you go on a journey of discovery together. Establishing a productive working relationship with your tutor will be very important.

Below are some ideas of what you can do to ensure you get the most out of your tutor:

- Be organised, friendly and grateful to the tutor for sharing knowledge and experience with you.
- Take initiative and be proactive.
- Share your thought process and working methods with the tutor as precisely as possible.
- Always make an appointment in advance to see your tutor, giving a few options of when you are available. If you can no longer make the appointment, cancel it. Trying to re-book the appointment for the same time the following week often works well.

- Always go to a tutorial prepared.
- Ideally, send an up-to-date outline or a new draft chapter to the tutor in advance of the tutorial, preferably a week beforehand to give the tutor plenty of time to read and reflect on your work.
- For practice-based research and creative practice, share online video links with your tutor, showing excerpts of your work-in-progress. Alternatively, bring your notes or a draft to the meeting or arrange for the tutor to watch excerpts of work-in-progress in the studio or on screen, so that you have something concrete to talk about.
- Make a list of topics or questions you wish to discuss with the tutor.

Drafts

Showing your tutor draft writing is a unique opportunity to get feedback on your work that is impossible to gain by other means. Not all universities or colleges offer the opportunity to get feedback on draft work, due to institutional pressures on staff time and the need to create parity of experience for all students. You may want to find out about the following:

- Does your university or college have a system in place for dissertation tutoring?
- What limitations exist in terms of the sections or number of versions that can be submitted?
- What are the deadlines set by the tutor?
- If no dissertation tutoring support is available, what alternatives are there, for example through general learning support and development services and language centres?

In any case, you must do everything within your power to benefit from any support that is on offer for reviewing draft work-in-progress. The process of writing works best when it is iterative, meaning that you will need to revisit what you have written and develop it over time. There is a kind of meticulous labour involved in clarifying the structure of your text, strengthening your line of argument and developing the effectiveness of your written communication.

A tutor will act as a first reader of your work and can provide comments about sections that need clarification and arguments that are not yet persuasive and need to be strengthened with additional evidence. In this capacity, the tutor will probably not explain how exactly you can fix these problems, as this requires your own independent initiative. You may not have a second chance to show a new version to the tutor, so it is important to drill down deeply into the problem and implement a fix that thoroughly addresses the root of the issue.

A tutor can also pick up on language errors or habitual patterns in your writing that are likely to distract the reader from your discussion and argument. However, it is not reasonable to expect that the tutor will 'correct' all your spelling, grammatical or stylistic errors; instead, expect the tutor to point out the broad principles of what needs to be changed for you to carefully review and improve your own writing. This is a valuable learning process for your professional future. Working closely with a tutor on your writing as is characteristic for a dissertation is potentially the only opportunity you will ever have to improve your writing through such an intensive process, so make sure you address the feedback independently and meticulously.

When getting ready to submit draft work for feedback, try to push yourself to get your work to a suitable standard. Of course, it will not yet be perfect, but nevertheless you should commit to developing your work to a level with which you are reasonably happy, for the moment. This means:

- developing your paragraphs from outline to prose form
- attaching a properly formatted bibliography, so that the tutor can see which source materials you have been working with so far.

You should be able to find out when you can reasonably expect feedback on your work. Of course, it is of crucial importance to carefully consider, address and implement the tutor's feedback. Nothing is more frustrating for a tutor than to spend time giving detailed and constructive feedback and subsequently discovering in a next or final draft that the student has ignored it.

Study support services

There may be an opportunity in your university or college for general support with your studies. The staff working in these services are not subject specialists and are unable to offer subject-specific guidance. However, they are skilled in helping students to establish productive working patterns and can help you to develop strategies for time management, structuring your ideas and communicating them more effectively in your writing. You may gain new skills and develop your existing skills by exploring group workshops or individual study support while working on your dissertation.

Peer support

Completing an independent research project such as a dissertation can be a lonely endeavour. Some of you might feel isolated in attempting to conquer this major academic challenge at a time when you may have fewer scheduled group sessions in which to share questions, ideas and approaches about this assignment with other students compared to previous years. You may be able to find support throughout the challenge of the dissertation project with your peers, through formal learning activities set up by your university or college, such as research seminars, or informally through your own initiative, such as study groups.

It can be useful to talk about your research ideas and progress with peers at various stages in the process.

- Sometimes, simply voicing your questions and dilemmas to others can help you to find solutions about how to move forward.
- Fellow students may have useful reading suggestions for your research or suggest libraries and online databases that you might want to explore.
- Sometimes, simply hearing that other students are facing different but equivalent challenges in their research can help to put you at ease about your own struggles. You can strengthen each others' confidence that you will be able to overcome them successfully.

However, when sharing work with your peers, you must carefully consider the need to avoid collusion, a form of academic misconduct. Collusion means working together with another student, or copying another student's work, and subsequently presenting that work as your own. Further explanations can be found in the regulations governing academic misconduct of your university or college. It is your responsibility to find out what is acceptable behaviour and what is not. Your tutor can advise you if necessary.

Working with research participants

Ethics

Whenever you are working with human participants in your research, you must carefully consider research ethics. Working with human participants includes interviews, questionnaires, observation or experiments involving yourself and/or other volunteer participants. You are responsible for the safety of your research participants. Therefore, as a researcher you must take steps to minimise the risks of physical, psychological and emotional harm to those participating in your research.

It is your responsibility to:

- familiarise yourself and comply with the regulations and formal procedures governing research ethics at your university or college
- ensure that any research findings are held in a secure environment and computerised records are password protected, in order to comply with data protection legislation.

Good practice in this area includes:

- submitting an ethics form to a dedicated panel
- producing a participant information sheet
- acquiring informed consent from the participants (see below)
- carrying out a health and safety risk assessment.

It is important for any research participant to enter into the arrangement of generating data or findings for your research knowingly and voluntarily. It is generally considered unethical to conduct research secretly, unbeknown to the participants. **Informed consent** is the term used to describe the process of research participants giving their permission for you to use the data and findings generated by their participation for the purposes of your research. The participants will also need to know if, how and where your research findings will be disseminated. Informed consent is usually obtained by asking your participants to sign a form. Your university or college might have a template for such a form; alternatively, you need to research the requirements on your own.

Extra care must be taken of participants who are considered vulnerable, such as children, people with learning difficulties, disabilities or mental health issues, the elderly, and people who have been the victim of a trauma or crime. It may be necessary to obtain informed consent from the person's parent, carer or legal guardian for participation in the research. You may need to consider alternatives if consent cannot be gained. Perhaps, instead of observing a dance practice session or speaking to participants directly, it may be possible to speak to the workshop leader instead.

Concerns have been raised in the field about whether working with dancers as part of a practice-based research project constitutes a similar need to consider research ethics. The principles of informed consent could be considered to apply just the same there. It is good practice to inform the dancers with whom you plan to work not only of rehearsal times, but also about specific ideas and creative processes you plan to explore, particularly if these are unusual. Are you planning to work with personal stories or memories shared by the performers in the creative process? Do you intend to explore and push the boundaries of exhaustion or extreme emotions? It can be argued that performers need to know about that in advance. That way, the dancers can make an informed decision about whether or not to work with you on your research.

Interviews

If you are using questionnaires or conducting interviews, it may be necessary for your tutor to sign off the questions in advance. In any case, it is useful to have the tutor's feedback in preparation for the questionnaire or interview.

If you plan to interview someone, it may be a good idea to send a few questions in advance to give the interviewee a chance to think ahead, unless there is a specific reason as to why that is not appropriate. You might need to research different approaches to interviewing; usually, a semi-structured interview works well, meaning you have a number of pre-existing questions that you would like to ask the person, but there is still room for the conversation to develop naturally.

When planning and conducting your interview, you should carefully consider the types of question you pose. Open-ended questions, using the words 'what', 'how' or 'why', for example, aim to generate a longer response, while closed questions are usually answered only with yes or no, or a short sentence. Clearly, open-ended questions are likely to lead to more interesting answers in an interview. However, that does not mean that your questions need to be very long or complicated. If you have posed a question and were hoping for a longer answer from your interviewee, you can ask for clarification and/or dig a little deeper with a follow-up question.

Interviewing people is a skill that needs to be developed. Good listening skills are, of course, paramount, so that the interviewee understands that you are really listening to and connecting with the insights being offered up in the conversation. Always make it clear whether the conversation will be recorded and how you will use that recording in your research. You may decide that it is necessary to transcribe the interview in its entirety and include it in your dissertation as an appendix. If it is not possible to interview someone in person, telephone or online video platforms may offer a good alternative. Additionally, answering your questions by email may be a last resort, although there is, of course, much less possibility of following up on the person's responses.

If the person you want to interview is a well-known artist or leadership figure, it may be hard to get that person to agree to being interviewed due to a busy schedule. The key is to make your request for an interview stand out, by displaying an already thorough knowledge and understanding of the person's work and achievements, and of any published interviews already given. Public figures may grant your request more easily if there is mutual value in holding the conversation; they may agree to it if your research questions are interesting and can help shed light on a particular aspect of their work or practice.

Focus point

This former student describes what she did to secure an interview with contemporary ballet choreographer Crystal Pite:

As soon as I encountered Crystal Pite's work, initially on YouTube and later in the theatre, I immediately became inspired and knew that I would want to find out more about her and her work. Hence, when deciding on a dissertation topic, it didn't take me long to land on Pite's work as a central focus. From my initial research, reading reviews of her works and listening to online interviews, I became particularly interested in the role of text and narrative in Pite's work, and how this works with the choreographic and visual aspects that she creates.

It became clear that my research would become better if I could have access to video recordings of some of Pite's works and if I could pose her questions about my research interests directly. However, I was aware that my requests for these could easily be turned down for various reasons. She and her collaborators no doubt have very busy schedules. Pite might also not want to run the risk of making video recordings of her work available to members of the public.

Therefore, when approaching Pite through the email address of her assistant available on her website, I made sure to convey the following:

- a very brief introduction, including where I was studying, at what level and on what course
- my intense interest in Pite's work, and which aspects of her work I wanted to investigate in particular for my dissertation
- a reference to online interviews with Pite, to reassure her that I had already explored all the materials that were in the public domain
- a request for video recordings of specific works, with the reassurance that I would not share these materials with anybody. I offered to pay for the costs of sending.
- a request for an interview, including the kinds of questions I would like to pose.

Shortly after sending this email, I received a reply from Pite's assistant, saying that Pite supported giving access to her work to researchers and that the requested DVDs were in the post. Unfortunately, it was not possible to organise a face-to-face interview due to logistical and time reasons, but Pite would be very happy to answer my questions by email. While this was not exactly the outcome I had hoped for – and my dream of meeting her in person would not come true – I was very understanding of the situation. The responses that Pite sent to my questions were detailed and extremely helpful to my dissertation.

Commonly used research terminology

In conducting your research, you might encounter generic research terminology used across disciplines. Some common research-related terms are outlined below, but it is worth noting that different disciplines may have their various sensibilities, definitions or treatments of the terms.

- **Secondary sources** are produced by other voices in the field that you as a student engage with. This can include documents, such as books and journals, research papers, official/organisational publications and statistics, media including sound, photography and film, newspapers, web sources and artefacts.
- **Primary sources** will be the research and resulting material produced by you in direct response to your inquiry. This can include data gathered through observation, questionnaires and research experiments, the outcomes of analysis and/or interviews, and your own reflection.
- **Qualitative** forms of data are focused on description and are text-based. Different qualitative methods can be employed, such as descriptive accounts, journaling, written reflection, reports, observations, questionnaires, transcribed interviews and focus groups.
- **Quantitative** forms of data are numeric, mathematical, presented in a graph/table and statistics, such as polls. These quantitative methods can involve calculation and measurement, using questionnaires and other experimental research concerned with testing variables, analysing and interpreting data, and looking for patterns and anomalies.
- **Deductive approaches** refer to your engagement with existing hypotheses, rules, models and your application and testing out of these. The key point about deductive research is that the rule, model or hypothesis already exists.
- **Inductive approaches** involve the generation of an argument or theory from your engagement with a particular phenomenon, situation, event, behaviour or concept. The key point about inductive research is that this approach starts out broad and gradually focuses in towards a more honed argument.

Not all of these terms will be relevant to your dissertation project. You should ensure that you understand the research terminology that you encounter as your research unfolds. You might like to begin to keep a glossary in your process journal, so that you can gather definitions of any important, recurring terms that are new to you.

Managing source material

Library and research skills

Your institutional library will hold a wealth of material: books, journal publications, online databases and e-publications. It is important to understand the various searches that can be carried out and develop appropriate strategies for accessing these sources. Your library may also be able to organise inter-library loans to obtain publications from other institutions.

Librarians can help you to develop the skills needed to navigate the university library's catalogue and online databases. They tend to run regular sessions about research skills, including how to use search terms in order to yield productive searches. Some libraries may hold specialised sessions for dissertation research. In the library, subject-specific readers and collected volumes are often a good place to start. The reference lists at the end of each chapter in these edited collections provide a good avenue of next steps to explore the topic in more depth.

Resources for research

Below is a list of the types of resources you should consider and explore as part of your research:

- **Books and other published materials:** There are general key texts in the various areas of interest in dance research, which often provide an introduction to the subject area and its components. These can be edited editions collating a series of essays or papers. The next step is to explore more specific texts dedicated to a more detailed research topic. Other published materials could include research reports, reviews, performance programmes and conference papers.
- **Scholarly, peer-reviewed journals:** Peer review means that the researched articles have gone through a rigorous process of review by eminent and active scholars from that particular specialist area. A particular dance area may have a dedicated journal, such as the examples listed below. However, this is by no means an exhaustive list:
  - *Journal of Dance Medicine & Science* ISSN 1089-313X
  - *Journal of Music and Dance* ISSN: 2360–8579
  - *Journal of Dance & Somatic Practices* – ISSN: 17571871
  - *Dance Research Journal* ISSN: 01497677
  - *Journal of Dance Education* ISSN: 1529-0824
  - *Choreographic Practices* ISSN: 20405669.

  Common online databases for journals in dance and related fields include:
  - International Bibliography of Theatre and Dance
  - JSTOR
  - SPORTDiscus.
- **Practical classes, workshops and conferences:** Acquiring research material from practice is also an acceptable source. Material can be gathered through printed hand-outs, experiential journals and notes on a dance practice or process. There may be a conference aiming to share new research in the field you are looking at. Your supervisor may be able to advise you about relevant events.
- **Bibliographies and reference lists at the end of source material:** If you have a particular topic of research where you feel there is little material, but manage to get hold of one article, take a glance at the bibliographic or reference list, as this can be extremely helpful in locating associated material. This is often helpful if your area crosses into other disciplines, for example, dance and technology or dance and social sciences.
- **Web sources:** Google Scholar and Google Books can provide useful access to reliable web resources. The web addresses of academic articles and papers often end in [.edu] or [.ac.uk]. Online resources might include dance company websites, artist or practitioner blogs, organisation sites, research papers, articles and reviews. Online resources might also include other modes of research, such as film and sound in the form of documentation, recorded performance, dance film, conference presentations and interviews by

professionals. Unreliable sources need to be avoided. You should critically assess online sources for validity.

Staying on top of a vast amount of research

- When collecting research, put in place a well-structured system to file the material, both on your computer and in hard copy, if appropriate.
- Keep a complete record of the sources you have consulted for the bibliography and keep track of the sources of information, ideas or material that you are considering using in your dissertation, including the chapter and page number. This will not only ensure you have all the information you need to reference the source accurately, but it will also enable you to refer back to the precise place in a source to check back over something at a later stage.
- Organise the research you have gathered and prioritise what you will need to read immediately and what can wait until a later stage.
- Consider using quick reading techniques, such as scanning (looking out for a particular term or name) and skimming (reading diagonally to get a general impression of the content of a section), in order to identify which particular texts you will need to read slowly and in detail.
- When reading in detail, try to be actively engaged in the process by making notes, highlighting important points, looking up things you do not understand and making connections with other things you have read.

Bibliographies and referencing

It is of the utmost importance to keep careful track of the sources you are using for your research. These include books, journal articles, newspaper and magazine articles, websites, films, documentaries, TV programmes, interviews, live performances, music recordings and scores, and so on. Failure to meticulously reference the sources you have used in your dissertation will most likely result in plagiarism or academic misconduct. Your university or college will be forced to award serious penalties when this is discovered, such as failure or expulsion. Therefore, you must do everything in your power to avoid plagiarising inadvertently through a lack of understanding of the need to reference sources and the academic conventions surrounding the issue.

You must adhere to the referencing system required by your university or college. Depending on the system, you will either have in-text citations, footnotes or endnotes in the text of your dissertation to indicate precisely where you refer to existing knowledge and arguments that have already been published. There will be guidelines about the system your university or college uses, and you may be able to get support with implementing the guidelines in your own coursework. Referencing software such as Ref Me and other embedded word processing databases can capture source information, or provide a template for you to input this. These helpful electronic systems can construct your bibliography and reference list too, as well as advise on in-text referencing. You would need to know your university's own system to use these.

It is important to represent direct quotations appropriately to indicate that these are not your own words, but have been written or spoken by someone else. Usually, the quoted text will be placed between quotation marks within your continuous text for brief quotations, or indented and single-spaced for longer quotations.

Where you have changed the published text into your own words – paraphrasing – you must still acknowledge the source of the material with an in-text citation, foot-note or endnote. So, even though you have changed the precise wording, you must still acknowledge who had the idea in the first place. Not knowing that somebody else had published the idea previously is not an excuse; it is your job as a student to read and find out as much as possible in your research area, and therefore to know what the main thoughts are about the topic as published in the field. Not knowing that other people had already published the same idea as you had, is referred to as cryptomnesia, or imagining that an already existing thought is new and original. It is, of course, important to take reasonable steps as a student to avoid this happening.

It is important to understand that paraphrasing means more than simply replac-ing a few words in the source text with synonyms; instead, it is necessary to also substantially alter the sentence structure and perhaps the level of detail. Paraphrasing is a challenging skill, which takes time and needs plenty of practice; however, it is often preferred over the use of direct quotations because it will challenge you to make sure you have fully understood the material before you can rephrase it com-petently in your own words.

Is it necessary to reference general information and common knowledge? If a fact is well known and widely accepted, then it is not necessary to reference a source. However, it is not always easy to determine if a fact is common knowledge or not. It is also important to distinguish between a fact and an idea; ideas do need to be attributed to an author. If you are in doubt, it is always better to err on the side of caution and provide a citation anyway.

Also, see the section in Chapter 4 on discursive writing style for guidance about how to weave other authors' voices into your own writing and how to engage in a critical dialogue with these voices.

Coming to the end of this chapter, we recommend that you spend time com-pleting the following key activity.

Activity: Organising your research

Create your own timeline from inception of your dissertation idea through to completion, perhaps on a week-by-week calendar. You might prefer to do this on paper or using an electronic diary. If you use paper, leave plenty of space for changes and amendments.

- Mark the submission deadline and, working backwards, mark a period of one or two weeks to edit, proofread and bind your dissertation.
- Mark the date when the proposal is due and when you expect to receive approval. If you will need ethics approval for working with other people as participants in your research, determine what the timeframe is for that and mark the deadline onto your timeline.
- Identify what support mechanisms you can benefit from: tutorials, draft submissions and research and writing skills workshops. Map them onto your timeline, so that you are clear about your own interim deadlines for draft chapters.

- Map your other assessment work onto the timeline.
- Identify when you will have substantial periods of time to work on the dissertation and when you will be preoccupied with other activities. It is likely that you will have many weeks that are somewhere in between: you will have other things going on, but also some breaks in your schedule that will allow you to work on the dissertation for a few hours.
- Break the dissertation task up into smaller research and writing tasks, and map these smaller tasks and milestones to your timeline. Be prepared to be very flexible in adjusting this timeline as a result of new directions your research project might take or structural changes you might need to make to your document. However, always keep an eye on the bigger picture and make sure you keep the project on track.

Conquering your demons

Sometimes, psychological pressures can get the better of you and hinder your progress with your research project. This can be unexpected and scary, but it happens to quite a few students. There is a lot at stake with the dissertation; your ability to graduate may depend on it. The dissertation is probably also the most substantial project you will have taken on so far in your academic career, and it may be the longest text that you will have ever written. Added to this, the dissertation is an independent project, in which you will need to make your own decisions, and you are solely responsible for ensuring you are making progress over a substantial period of time. This combination can at times become an explosive cocktail of dark thoughts and a lack of self-belief that can result in mental health issues and even bouts of depression.

Therefore, it is important to recognise the warning signs when you are struggling to cope productively with the pressure that you are under. Seek help from friends, family or professional support services if things are getting really bad. Sometimes talking to someone can help put things into perspective and help you see a way forward.

Procrastination

Procrastination means avoiding tasks by doing other activities instead. It can also mean carrying out less urgent tasks first, instead of more important and urgent ones. It is not straightforward to explain or adjust procrastinating behaviour, and this book certainly does not pretend to hold all the answers. There is a wealth of online articles about procrastination, and attempting to find answers in them while you are meant to work on your dissertation is surely the most ironic form of procrastination. Nevertheless, it can help to research the problem at another time or to talk about the problem to someone, a friend, partner, family member, counsellor or doctor.

- Keeping a diary about your thoughts can also help you to understand your working habits, environment and preferences, and when procrastination is most likely to happen.
- Where are you most productive: in the library, at your desk at home, at the dinner table or in a busy café?

- Do you need to have music on, and if so, what kind? For some, instrumental or electronic music without words works well. Or do you need it to be absolutely quiet?
- Are you alone or with others? Dancers are often drawn to social learning situations, making it hard to be left alone with their thoughts and work on their own.
- What do you tend to be distracted by: people interrupting your flow of thought, phone calls, social media alerts, emails, construction noises?
- What kind of food or drink do you need to function well? Feeling hungry is likely to be a major distraction, but heavy meals are likely to make you feel tired. Coffee can make you alert, but keeping hydrated by drinking plenty of water will ensure you can keep focused for longer.

Once you have identified factors that are likely to lead you to procrastinate, think about how to take action to address the problem. How can you minimise distractions during the hours you have identified as working time? Switch off your mobile phone for a while; make sure someone else is on call to deal with family or other emergencies on your behalf. Your friends and family will understand and want to support you in successfully completing the dissertation, so let them know what you need from them. Making sacrifices like these to ensure an optimal, healthy working environment for yourself is definitely worth it. Even if you end up being not as productive as you had hoped this time around, you will have trained your brain to be focused on the task at hand and any progress, no matter how small, is a step in the right direction and should be celebrated.

Sometimes it can be hard to get into the swing of researching, thinking and writing. You may find that it takes you some time to get your head back into the material when you have been away from it for a while. Re-reading past work or consulting a plan or outline can help to get you into the right headspace. It is not always possible in your schedule to work for substantial periods of time in one go. You may not have entire days to work on the dissertation. In that case, it can be useful to identify short blocks of time in your diary when you can work on the project, an hour, an evening, a train journey or a break in your schedule. By working on the project frequently, even for short bursts of time, you are likely to retain your flow and swing of thinking more easily. The length of time you can concentrate on a single task will vary for everyone. You will need to take regular breaks, ideally involving some fresh air and gentle exercise or stretching.

Try not to feel guilty or beat yourself up after individual bouts of procrastination. Even if you lose a day, or longer, all is not lost and it is almost always possible to put the project back on track. What is done is done, and cannot be changed. The key is to park the negative feelings and move forward positively. Swiftly adjust your working plan and timeline, re-prioritise your tasks and visualise a healthier working process.

Finding good quality motivation and flow

Motivation is the driving force that makes you pursue hard and challenging work. Sometimes, you may feel as if you are lacking motivation to pursue your dissertation research. However, it may be helpful to stop thinking of motivation as something that you need more of, in terms of quantity, and instead try to understand what makes for good quality motivation. Psychologists often make a distinction between extrinsic and intrinsic motivation to indicate whether the motivation arises from outside or inside the individual. Extrinsic motivation means that your actions are driven by a desire to earn a reward – in the case of the dissertation, for example, to get a good grade. Intrinsic motivation means that you do something because you find a sense of enjoyment in the activity itself and the challenge, in other words, working on your dissertation research for the sake of it. Another way of thinking about it is that some individuals tend to be more focused on the end goal of an activity, whereas others are more intent on enjoying the process.

Flow is a concept used in positive psychology to identify a state of being when you find yourself in an optimal zone of performance, sometimes described as losing yourself in the activity. When you achieve flow, you forget about other aspects of your life for a while. It may seem as if time flies by without you having realised you have been working for hours. Being in a state of flow is often associated with dance, and it is easy to understand why. However, it could be really useful to think about being in a state of flow when researching and writing your dissertation. When it happens, it will be much easier for you to find the joy of the process of dissertation research, associated with intrinsic motivation.

Finding your confidence

Your dissertation project is a worthwhile endeavour that a number of people will find interesting and rewarding. You are devoting a significant amount of time and effort to this research and it will result in interesting insights that are worth being communicated. You might disseminate some of the research more widely, for example through an online blog.

During the writing process, it will be key to develop confidence in your own scholarly voice and the argument you wish to convey.

- What is it that you would like the reader to understand differently about the topic?
- How will you build a case for this argument and what evidence will you need to persuade the reader?

By carefully considering these questions and the guidance in Chapter 4 throughout the writing process, and employing your own self-critical eye to interrogate the standards of your work, you can feel more confident about the quality of your work and your ability to meet this major challenge.

While there are ways to increase the readership of your research, the main benefits of the dissertation research process are for you personally. The skills you will develop throughout the project will help you to attain a higher level of academic skills and maturity, as well as life skills that are transferable more widely. The kind of behaviours that are stimulated through the dissertation – inquisitiveness, making connections between concepts, forging new insights and communication – are great ways of being in the world more generally. By engaging with the dissertation as an opportunity to develop your confidence in your own thoughts and voice, you will not only become a better professional, but also a better citizen and person who can make a contribution to the world around you.

Student comments:

'What support did you take advantage of?'

'My dissertation supervisor during this process was someone who was very knowledge-able in the area that I was researching. I spoke to her about ideas I was having, so that we could discuss the different ways in which these could be approached.'

'I made sure that I always had work to show my tutor when I met her, so that we had something to discuss.'

'During my research, I made sure I attended all the instruction sessions and lectures. This gave me the opportunity to talk through my ideas and research methods with my peers and project co-ordinator.'

'I would not have managed to finish my dissertation by the hand-in day without interim submission points. These points gave me a clear guideline to organise my writing pace.'

'I met my dissertation tutor regularly, making sure I always arrived with questions so I could get a lot out of my tutorials.'

Summary points:

Divide the project into small, manageable tasks and set your own interim deadlines.

Adopting a reflective approach to the research process will help you to self-manage your dissertation project. Keep a process journal in which you record your thought process about how your research is taking shape.

Make use of the tutorial support system on offer at your university or college. Submitting draft work is an essential opportunity to gain feedback on your dissertation. Ensure you thoroughly address the feedback in your next version.

Research ethics must be carefully considered when working with human participants (interviews, questionnaires, observation, experiments, etc.). You must obtain informed consent from all participants in your project.

Meticulously managing source material is vitally important, both for managing your own time to work through the material and for enabling yourself to compile the bibliography and use the referencing system required by your university or college.

Psychological pressures can become a hindrance and lead to procrastination. Don't let these get the better of you. Evaluate the quality of your motivation and aim to find a state of flow when researching and writing your dissertation.

Chapter 3

Thinking on your feet: the research process

Chapter outline:

Methods and methodology

Thinking on your feet metaphorically indicates that you are ready for action and prepared to shift perspective or alter direction at a moment's notice. Thinking on your feet perhaps also implies that you have a selection of tools ready to hand for a variety of situations. In gesturing towards a set of tools, we want to actively guide you through potential approaches to research practice. There are a variety of research methods and theoretical perspectives available to you as a dance researcher in a number of clusters of interest. For example, clusters include choreography, cultures, performance, and media and technology. The overview of these clusters of interest in this chapter will help you to further refine your own research project in a way that makes best use of the methods and perspectives to deepen your inquiry.

This chapter introduces and explains how you might go about selecting a methodology and methods for your research project. A simple web search using the term 'methodology' reveals the extent to which others have attempted to define this term in various academic disciplines and in more general terms; hence, this term can be the cause of distinct confusion and contrasting ideas and approaches. The term 'methodology' is also often confused with the root term 'method'. However, these are not the same thing.

Research methods are simply the activities that you as the researcher undertake as part of your research and they exist as part of your methodology. In Table 3.1 we have listed commonly used dance research methods. Research any that seem relevant to your inquiry in more depth through your independent research.

Your methodology also includes the theoretical framework, concepts and perspectives that you are using to make sense of your research findings, in other words, the lens through which you look at the research.

More simply put, the methodology can be seen as an umbrella term for all the research methods you have employed during the research and the theoretical framework, concepts and perspectives that you have drawn on in shaping your project. A variety of methods can be used depending on your inquiry and you could adopt a 'mixed methods' approach. You will need to detail a rationale for why this is necessary. Talk this through with your tutor for clarity.

Table 3.1 Research methodology

Research methods	Theoretical framework
• literature review	• theories
• performance analysis	• philosophies
• interview	• concepts
• questionnaire	• perspectives
• observation	• other scholars' work
• reflection	
• focus group	
• documentary/film making/ media work	
• journaling/blogging	
• practice-as-research	
• performance	
• workshop/classes	
• improvisation	
• constructing a narrative	
• dramaturgy	
• laboratory testing	
• archival research	

There are established methodologies that are typical for particular academic disciplines. This chapter will explain the ones typical for dance, outlining key clusters of interest that characterise the discipline. It will become clear that different areas of dance research can be approached through multiple methodologies, reflecting differing perspectives on the topic. Common methodologies in dance may be based on a range of philosophies, such as phenomenology and feminism, scholarly disciplines such as anthropology, social science and performance, alongside the more experimental and survey methodologies related to science subjects. Each of these serves to provide a particular perspective on dance and the body, uncovering a unique kind of knowledge and encompassing a distinct approach.

Other guides to dissertation research might specify that you discuss your methodology in a distinct and dedicated chapter. However, in some dance research projects you may be encouraged to structure your dissertation creatively without the use of prescribed headings, as will be discussed in Chapter 4 of this book. Nevertheless, even if you do not include a dedicated methodology chapter in your dissertation, it is still important to demonstrate your awareness of your methodology either in the introduction or first chapter embedded in your dissertation. In this way, you will be explaining to your reader how you have gone about your research, justifying and giving a rationale for your chosen approach.

Your research methodology should be appropriate and effective for achieving the particular aims of your research. There should be a sense of continuity in your project as a whole. The decisions you make about your research methods and theoretical framework should be guided by a good understanding of the field and a clear vision for what you are aiming to achieve in your project. For example, a scientific experiment with numeric or short form yes/no data may not make sense if you are looking to uncover a complex and detailed understanding of dance as a cultural practice. Ask yourself primarily what it is that your inquiry is seeking to uncover and, correspondingly, what is the most effective way of achieving those outcomes.

To sum up, your methodology contains your research methods (what you have done) and theoretical framework (what you have used to make sense of your findings). It also consists of your reflection on the reasons for your decision making. It may be discussed in a separate chapter in your dissertation or it may be embedded in your introduction and/or opening chapter. A discussion of your methodology may also form part of other documents, such as reports, proposals and reflections. It may also be presented verbally through presentation or viva voce (see Chapter 4).

Sometimes articulating your methodology is about the process of shaping the design of your project as you are doing it, making adjustments and refining as you go along. This is to be expected and encouraged. You may find that keeping a process journal or notebook will help you to document and reflect on the research process as you are doing it. Often it can be a process of adjusting focus between carrying out the research and stepping back to reflect on what you did to build an overview.

Some institutions may require you to outline your methodology earlier in the project, by a given deadline. Often this task will follow a contextual literature or field review, so it is good to restate your topic, inquiry or question at the start of your methodology as an introduction. However, having to state and commit to a methodology at an early stage does not mean that it is completely set in stone. Rather, maintaining a continually reflective approach is vital in facilitating the small shifts that your project may need to achieve its aims, as you keep deepening and refining your research.

Some established methodologies

It is important to recognise that methodologies in dance research often incorporate interdisciplinary perspectives and methods borrowed from other scholarly disciplines, as well as more specifically focused forms of research and ways of thinking, developed through dance scholarship itself. Whilst it is not possible to go into depth about all methodologies open to you, in this section we highlight a number of established methodologies in dance research. It is useful to consider these when aligning your dissertation project with the suggested clusters of interest, which we outline later in this chapter.

Analysis

Analysis means breaking something up into smaller parts or elements, in order to examine the material in detail and gain an understanding of how it is structured. As a methodology for dance research, analysis may be guided by the use of a specific analytical method or model to focus on a particular aspect of the material you have selected for your inquiry. Alternatively, you might take a more integrated approach, drawing on a range of analytic perspectives simultaneously. The themes for exploration might well be uncovered as you analyse. The purpose of analysis in dissertation research is to identify the key elements that make up the research material and examine relationships between these elements. This will enable you to discuss the research findings in depth and use a critical approach.

There are various interdisciplinary approaches to analysis in dance research, such as cultural, historical and scientific analysis. Debates have been held in dance research about the importance of movement-focused analysis to make clear the centrality of dance as a language of gesture. Analytical approaches specific to dance have been developed, such as Laban Movement Analysis (Newlove and Dalby 2004), Adshead's Dance Analysis model (1988), and Preston-Dunlop and Sanchez-Colberg's Nexus model (2002). These dance-specific analytical approaches pay particular attention to movement description and the relationships between elements within the dance or movement examined. Methods might involve viewing a performance or process (live or recorded) and using a structured approach to note down material, which is then interpreted and discussed. Some models have a structured chart-based approach that should be followed to record performance information. Comparisons and correlations can then be made between analyzed examples of work.

Scientific approaches might measure numeric forms of data and structure these to arrive at results. Tabled formats are often used to display both qualitative and quantitative data appropriate to the model used. Discussion will often draw on tabled information to interpret and illuminate the findings in relation to relevant theoretical perspectives weaved into the analysis.

If you are considering analysis for your research project, you should carefully consider the selection of material for analysis and the approach(es) or model(s) that you will use. Articulate a rationale for the choices made. It would be helpful to do this with your tutor.

Ethnography

Ethnography is a research methodology for exploring different cultures and subcultures. There are also the associated terms autoethnography (based on self-reflection and personal experience) and netnography (based on online interactions and digital communication). Dance ethnography focuses on movement practices in different societies. Taking a cultural approach to dance research can contribute to knowledge about the beliefs and values of a specific culture.

Ethnography typically involves 'field' research. The researcher collates qualitative material about the dance practice in its cultural setting through an experiential account of being in that field. It can involve observation, participant-observation, interviews (unstructured), case studies and focus groups. Collated material or field notes will be sorted and coded by themes that can then be discussed in relation to relevant theory and other cultural research.

Care should be taken to recognise the researcher's own cultural biases and interests in the representation of the field. Reflecting on the way in which your own attitudes and ideas affect how you interpret the field can strengthen your critical examination of it.

Historiography

Historiography is a methodology that addresses how particular histories have been formed – in other words, how a particular version of history has come into being. A history of something is recounted through many voices and from different perspectives, leading to different emphases and sometimes conflicting views. As a result, what is considered historical 'fact' can be slippery and influenced by power relationships.

Historiographical research aims to interrogate this formation of history and redress the power balances in the representation of historical events. It often involves a direct engagement with source material, such as artefacts, documents, media and oral histories. By considering a range of historical accounts and source material in relation to a broader understanding of the cultural, social and/or political context of the period, the researcher can discuss what may have prompted particular accounts or viewpoints, enabling a critical examination of how a history has been formed.

For dance historiography, there are debates around the way in which dance has been documented throughout history, what voices are included or left out of historic accounts and how choreographies and movement practices can be articulated, preserved and passed on for restaging or reworking.

Action research

Action research happens in the context of a particular practice in which the researcher is active. It is designed to identify issues and provide solutions that are tested out through active participation. Reflexive practice encourages the researcher to reflect on what has taken place in order to develop any future activity in an informed way.

Commonly used in, but not limited to, educational and community research, this approach relies on an identification of a particular issue or problem within a participatory setting, in order to reflect on how processes can be evolved, adjusted and developed to serve the needs of participants. This might involve the development of specific learning and teaching tools and the generation of strategies for assessment, feedback and evaluation. The research can take the form of a collaborative project in which a group of individuals with different roles might be experiencing a variety of issues with a working process. The researcher may gather data in the form of process documents, case studies and/or discussion groups, so that all participants in the process are able to actively contribute to finding a solution.

With dance as an active and embodied practice, this approach to research takes account of what it is to work with the processes involved in practice. Action research isolates where such processes can evolve to meet the particular challenges and needs faced by those in an instructive, mentoring, learning and advisory role.

Phenomenology

Phenomenology arguably is a philosophy – not a methodology. It is incorporated in this section as it has formally been a common approach to research in dance. This is largely because its ideology challenges the mind and body split prompted by Cartesian philosophy ('I think, therefore I am' – in Latin: *Cogito ergo sum* (Descartes 1644)). Philosopher René Descartes' viewpoint reflects the assumption that the mind is separate from the body and thought is somehow more important than the experience of being. In contrast, phenomenology is concerned with the nature of phenomena as they are open to our direct experience. An experiential account is critically examined to take into consideration all that occurs within experience, not just perceptually, but all that occurs within our awareness and how this is structured. It does not rely on finding a singular truth, but addresses what might be important to the experienced accounts and why.

Dance revolves around experiential and embodied practice, which reflects an active relationship between thinking and doing. As such, dance has sought to emphasise this throughout its discipline and scholarship, attempting to erase this separation that has become a common understanding in contemporary culture. Experiential accounts can be extremely valuable to the study of dance. For instance, a leap in the air may be described in a particular way. We could identify it by suggesting a measured height or that both feet are in the air, but the sense of a leap in the experience of doing one carries a very different quality of description. It is this phenomenological description that is required in order to make an interpretation. Researchers can use numerous methods for collecting accounts, such as narrative response, participant observation and interviews.

Experimental research

Experimental research is largely used as an approach in dance science and follows the more traditionally established ways of thinking based on cause and effect. This particular research often involves the production of both qualitative and quantitative data and the use of established models of testing and analysis that pay particular attention to measurement, variables and statistics.

Often laboratory/studio based, this form of inquiry may involve designing your own experiment features based on the formalised testing of a focused sampling (potentially volunteers). Test results are then analysed as a central part of the research. Hypothesis testing, comparison, correlation, relationships and predicted outcomes should lead to a discussion of results. Strategies for dealing with statistical analysis could include scoring, addressing averages and variances.

Often this form of positivist research involves a concern for validity and reliability of data that can require a control experiment and survey methods. Experimental research can combine practical testing with some qualitative methods, such as case studies and focus groups. Ethics and informed consent are standard practice here (see Chapter 2).

Research philosophies

As researchers, our understanding and perhaps bias may influence our desire for a particular epistemology (type of knowledge and knowledge making within a field of study). This is related to how we form our thoughts, practices and beliefs about the world. Often, you will hold particular beliefs without question. However, being able to acknowledge and articulate the philosophical perspective that best fits your way of thinking will enable your audience to locate your approach. It is also part of the practice of critical thinking and doing.

This philosophy will play a part in how you research, in terms of the way you question or inquire about a topic, the methods you use and the way you carry these out. A scientist doing work in a laboratory will be concerned with adherence to experimental procedure in a controlled environment with potentially predictable outcomes. The educational researcher might need to observe teaching in action in a classroom situation. The feminist researcher will be critically questioning patriarchal values within the context of their study through the use of particular feminist theory and practice. The choreographic researcher might work with and through movement exploration to evolve new processes or theories. For each researcher, these approaches could be established ways of working and collecting particular data within that specific area or field. However, the research design is also aligned to disciplinary beliefs about what counts as research and knowledge. Dance researchers have broadened and valued the variety of knowledge forms that now exist through scholarly activity in the discipline.

This brief section introduces you to the notion of research philosophies, in order to make you aware of their potential to add a further critical layer to your work. Whilst you would be expected to fully engage with this in postgraduate study, it is useful at undergraduate level to understand and demonstrate an awareness of the range of perspectives a researcher might adopt.

Below are examples of some common approaches you may wish to explore. In aligning yourself to any of the perspectives mentioned, you need to make sure you have considered and understood what the approach entails through your own independent research. It would be helpful to talk through these with your tutor.

- subjectivism
- positivism
- realism
- interpretivism
- structuralism
- humanism
- feminism
- constructivism.

The philosophical examples in the list above also include a variety of derivatives, such as postpositivism, with slight differences in the titles according to developments and advances made within the particular philosophies.

Clusters of interest in dance

Familiar bodies of existing dance research have highlighted particular areas worthy of study that we have termed *clusters of interest*. These clusters or research areas act as a starting point for research and assist the dance researcher to understand the scope of inquiry within a broader setting. In identifying these clusters of interest, we offer some basic defining features or ideas for inquiry and suggested introductory source materials, so that you can explore this research area independently. We wholeheartedly support overlap and merging of these areas and encourage a degree of fluidity where rigorous researching practices allow for the possibility of extension across clusters. These ideas about possible approaches and research methodologies that you might explore are not intended as an exhaustive list of ways of working, nor do they advocate a 'right' way of working. Instead, you will need to carefully reflect on your specific research design from its inception and through to completion in order to find the unique solutions your project requires.

Choreography

Whilst choreography is the term commonly used to refer to set dance movement, it can also be seen as a research tool and even a methodology. This would be the case when developing choreographies that directly address research inquiries. Because the term 'choreography' reaches beyond dance into other disciplines, it has broadened from dance to focus on organised movement as a more generalised principle. In this way, words, space, animals, people, time and objects are among some of the things that can be choreographed and can choreograph.

Research in choreography is a relatively new area in research, which historically has evolved from modern and postmodern dance practice and the early beginnings of dance education. Current debates exist around the development of choreographic forms, collaboration, ownership and definition. In researching choreography, the focus may be on creative process, teaching or pedagogical approaches and how choreography intersects with other disciplines. So, the context of your focus is important here for both defining your use of the term choreography and how it is of concern in a particular setting.

Research might focus on the specific style, form and content of a dance or attention might be paid to re-workings and re-stagings of established dances and themes to address the variety of expressions that exist. In dance practice, choreography can be explored through the lens of the creative processes involved in the work of your own practice and that of choreographers. You might engage with general, overarching questions that could be applied to any choreographic practice or specific questions could arise from concerns within your practice itself.

In dance education, choreography can be explored in terms of particular taught approaches and issues concerning learning and teaching. The focus might be on how specific forms of choreographic practice are passed on, which may have a bearing on their development.

Typically, research in choreography might include examining choreography using analytical tools and looking at how practice and creative outcomes might allow the choreographic inquiry to come to the fore. For example, a past student researched definitions of the term 'pedestrian', which led to the exploration and development of task-based choreographic methods for the purpose of generating pedestrian movement.

 Focus points

Key search terms: composition, intention, improvisation, choreographic tools, collaboration, re-working, re-staging, creative process, social choreography, praxis, documentation, authorship, inter-disciplinarity, task-based choreography, site-specific, site-based, site-adaptive choreography, style, technique, performance presence

Organisations: One Dance UK's Choreographers Directory, Ausdance, choreographiclab. org

Methodologies: choreography, performance analysis, ethnography, heuristics

Philosophical approaches and ideology: feminism, phenomenology, postcolonialism, identity politics, cultural theory

Publications:

> Midgelow, V.L. and Bacon, J.M. (eds.) *Choreographic Practices* journal, first published in 2010 and electronically available.
> Minton, S.C. (2007) *Choreography: A Basic Approach Using Improvisation.* 3rd edn, Champaign, IL: Human Kinetics.
> Green, D.F. (2010) *Choreographing From Within: Developing the Habit of Inquiry as an Artist.* Champaign, IL: Human Kinetics.
> Burrows, J. (2010) *A Choreographer's Handbook.* Abingdon, Oxon: Routledge.

Cultures

This research area focuses on the role of dance in a range of cultures and subcultures on a global scale. Inquiries stem from how moving bodies can reflect changes in culture and also how cultural events can reflect developments in movement forms including dance practice. Dance as a term within differing cultures is broad and shifting. It may be regarded as a form of expressive movement in space and time. It can be evidenced through ritual in religious and secular contexts, social practice, entertainment culture, political identity, sports, fitness, body language, signing and gesture.

Research is characterised by interests in the dancing body in different contexts and what dance or the dancer represents in terms of meaning, identity, values and politics. Generally, the cultural context you are researching is positioned as an 'other' to the researcher, but can at times involve self-reflective methods based on the researcher's own experiential account. Data is mostly qualitative and relies on the collection of detailed, 'rich' description that can be analysed and can highlight important findings relating to cultures as they are lived and practiced.

When researching in this area, you are likely to spend a substantial amount of time in the field that you choose. If the field is a particular taught dance genre, this could involve you attending regular dance classes either as participant or observer. Time spent in the field as observer/participant should be documented by journaling, note-taking and/or recording electronically with the necessary permissions sought. Other primary methods might include gathering artefacts or documents from the field, interviews and questionnaires. Once data has been gathered it is analysed through a coding of particular themes. Generating these themes can be done by going through the research material and isolating important information relating to your inquiry and highlighting areas that might be unusual, prompting alternative issues not previously considered. Initially you will be looking at the participants' behaviour and what is understood by those in the cultural setting.

- Are there particular roles that you can identify?
- What are the relationships between people and practices?
- What structures exists in that culture?

Researchers are generally interested in themes surrounding identity hierarchies, agency and power. Theoretical approaches might involve cultural theories surrounding these themes. Examples of student dissertation projects in this area include ethnographic studies of movement practices, e.g. Zumba, cheerleading, burlesque, club dance and Irish dance. These projects tend to involve students gathering data over a period of time on class attendance, culture and observation, description and reflection on movement practice and form. Discussion can be based around a comparison of primary data in relation to contextual research to highlight significant relationships to wider aspects of cultural practice.

 Focus points

Key search terms: agency, power, hegemony, visibility, value, politics, the body, dualism, identity, ethnicity, gender, race, nationality, class, sexuality, 'the other', self/other, alterity, otherness, vernacular, colonial, postcolonial, nationalism, orientalism

Organisations: Congress on Research in Dance (CORD), The Association of Dance of the African Diaspora (ADAD), Pop Moves

Methodologies: ethnography, auto-ethnography, netnography, historiography

Philosophical approaches and ideology: cultural theory, identity politics, feminism, postcolonialism, phenomenology

Publications:

Buckland, T.J. (1999) *Dance in the Field: Theory, Methods and Issues in Dance Ethnography*. Basingstoke: Palgrave Macmillan.

Dankworth, L.E. and David, A.R. (eds.) (2014) *Dance Ethnography and Global Perspectives: Identity, Embodiment and Culture*. Basingstoke: Palgrave Macmillan.

Davida, D. (2011) *Fields in Motion: Ethnography in the Worlds of Dance*. Ontario: Wilfrid Laurier University Press.

Dodds, S. (2011) *Dancing on the Canon: Embodiments of Value in Popular Dance*. Basingstoke: Palgrave Macmillan.

Thomas, H. (2003) *The Body, Dance and Cultural Theory*. Basingstoke: Palgrave Macmillan.

Grau, A. and Jordan, S. (eds.) (2000) *Europe Dancing: Perspectives on Theatre, Dance, and Cultural Identity*. London: Routledge.

Performance

It is often assumed that you will know what constitutes performance if you are researching dance. However, many definitions exist. Care should be taken in defining this for yourself, drawing on a series of definitions to identify your own understanding. There have been debates surrounding what constitutes a performance, since much of the everyday overlaps with performance in terms of actions and settings (e.g. reality genres). Performance in its broadest sense whether on stage, on screen or in social or street settings provides a fertile ground for research, and it is likely that you will be well prepared to undertake such a project in your course of study. You will have been introduced to key models and approaches for analysing and drawing on performance to inform a research inquiry, and the dissertation offers a good opportunity to employ and further develop these skills.

The selection of performances for researching will depend on a number of factors. It is advisable to narrow down the genre or style of dance, and the context in which it is performed – stage, screen or social setting. You might decide to look at one or more works by a single choreographer or dance artist, or you might decide to compare the work of different artists working in the same or different time periods. You may also be interested in a specific theme or focus that is explored by a series of companies or choreographers to address different approaches in representing it.

If a single viewing of a live work is the only access to the performance you will have, you will need to ensure that you keep detailed notes during and immediately after the performance, so that you have enough to go on in your research. In contrast, screen-based dance that is broadcast on television or available on commercial DVDs or on online video-sharing platforms offers the benefit that you can watch the dance multiple times.

In a dissertation, you may be expected to both apply and interrogate relevant theoretical perspectives. Most centrally in your research, you could choose to interpret the dance images and experiences for meaning. In doing so, it is useful to consider semiotic theory, borrowed from linguistics and adapted to performance by many dance scholars, to enrich your understanding of not only the meanings that are produced in the dance, but also the ways in which the production of meaning takes place.

- What are the dominant meanings that are communicated in the work?
- How might the spectator understand how to read these images?
- Are there narrative layers in the dance, and how are these constructed?
- What are the deeper, underlying meanings that can be read into the narrative itself?

You might be interested in exploring theoretical perspectives on the representation of the dancing body in relation to the selected dance work(s).

- How are gendered identities, masculinities and femininities constructed in the performance?
- What about racial, cultural and national identity?
- How do the choreographic layers work to construct meanings about the performers' or characters' identity?
- Are these layers of meaning hegemonic or subversive; how and why?

Researchers might, again, choose different ways of researching performance and these can lead to a variety of ways in which findings are represented. You might look at a selection of works in terms of their scenographic significance and choose to explore these aspects of scenography in a performance of your own research. Alternatively, you may wish to analyse a selection of online screen works and write up your interpretation and discussion through the creation of an online journal. This greatly depends on the options and requirements for the programme of study at your institution.

 Focus points

Key search terms: scenography, performativity, performance presence, semiotics, performance space, place and site, linearity and non-Aristotelian narrative, representation, mise-en-scène, intertexuality

Organisations: Center for Performance Research, Society for Dance Research (Choreographic Forum)

Methodologies: performance analysis, historiography, ethnography

Philosophical approaches and ideology: narrative and semiotic inquiry, modernism/postmodernism, feminism, phenomenology, identity politics, cultural theory, social anthropology in terms of defining performance

Publications:

Adshead, J. (ed.) (1988) *Dance Analysis: Theory and Practice*. London: Dance Books.
Counsell, C. and Wolf, L. (eds.) (2001) *Performance Analysis: An Introductory Coursebook*. London: Routledge.

Preston-Dunlop, V. (1998) *Looking at Dances: A Choreological Perspective on Choreography.* London: Verve Publishing.

Sörgel, S. (2015) *Dance and the Body in Western Theatre: 1948 to the Present.* London: Palgrave Macmillan.

Histories

The historical dimensions of a particular dance form or an artist's work can be a rich area for research. Valuable insights can emerge from investigating the relationship between dance and the wider historical context in which it takes place. Possible areas of focus could include the role that dance plays in the construction of national, racial, gendered and/or social class identity in a certain time and place. Similarly, productive research could emerge from investigating the interplay between major world events and the dance practices or work by dance artists with which they coincide. Through this approach, a viable research focus can be placed on the ways in which a particular dance practice both shapes and is shaped by its political, socio-economic and cultural context.

A key factor will be the need to delineate the research topic in time and space. It can be tempting to simply set out to research 'the history of' a particular dance practice, but broad investigations of this kind are unlikely to achieve the depth of discussion needed. Rather, it is advisable to significantly narrow down the focus of your research topic, so that your reading can be tailored accordingly. It may take a while to find the appropriate focus, so perhaps you need to allocate a particular period of time devoted to discovering what the most interesting issues are about the dance practice that you are broadly concerned with.

One of the challenges of researching a dance history related topic for your dissertation may be that, if there is already a wealth of secondary research published on the topic, it can seem that all that is left for you to do in your dissertation is to compile those insights that have already been published. However, while dance history is arguably the branch of dance studies that has been established the longest, there are still many under-researched areas that are worthy of being researched in more depth. In your dissertation, you can choose to find such a 'gap' in the literature: the work of an artist who may have been largely overlooked, a geographical focus that constitutes a blind spot in existing research, or a popular dance practice that has not yet been deemed worthy of serious scholarly consideration. While such a research project will undoubtedly be challenging, the reward that comes from overcoming the challenge of doing this kind of research will be great. All you need to do is make sure that you have carefully considered whether you have sufficient access to the source material needed to carry out an in-depth investigation. Sometimes, additional clues can be found by researching areas that are tangentially related to your selected research topic, such as discussions in another art form or field.

Moreover, as a dance student, you bring something extremely valuable to the research that other researchers previously may not have shared with you: an in-depth embodied understanding of dance that comes from training as a practitioner. Some published dance historical research has been developed by historians or artists working in fields other than dance, who have taken an interest in dance but may not have had a direct engagement with dance as an embodied practice. While taking care not to devalue the work of such scholars, building on the gaps left as a result of this can help to carve out a space for your own research, although any critiques of established research must be done fairly and sensitively.

A tip for employing your own embodied knowledge as a dancer to dance historical research is to add a direct engagement with the choreographic layers of primary source material to the examination of existing secondary publications. Primary sources have come into being during the time period under scrutiny, whereas secondary sources are created after the event in retrospect. Primary sources can include video recordings of dance, photographic materials, diaries and newspaper reviews. Secondary sources tend to be biographies, dance history books and documentaries, for example. The point here is that it always pays off to go back to and look closely at the dance, a video recording or photographs that reveal something about the kinesthetic qualities of the dance itself. However, when reviewing work that has lived on in the repertoire, think carefully about what it is exactly that you are seeing, as inevitably the work will have undergone some transformation over the years. By analysing directly the choreographic content of primary source material, you may find the process of researching more exciting, because it is possible to discover new insights that other scholars have not yet written about. Of course, it is important to survey the existing publications about the topic as well; this should go hand in hand with the analysis of primary source material.

Another thing to consider is whether you are completing a diachronic or a synchronic study of the dance practice at hand. Diachronic, here, refers to studying the development of dance through time, whereas synchronic means looking at a particular slice of time and what coincided with the dance at that particular time. In other words, a synchronic study investigates the events and art works in other forms that were synchronous with the dance, i.e. happened at the same time. The danger of only carrying out a diachronic study is that it will then appear that dance happened in a vacuum, unaffected by anything that went on around it. Another risk is that diachronic studies can lead to a version of events in which there is advancement or progress to a better or more interesting state of the art form (teleology), in the sense that in the past dance was less advanced, less complex, less interesting and therefore less good, compared to the more desirable state in which dance finds itself now.

In sum, it is advisable to always place the dance itself centrally in your discussion, to remove the emotion from the arguments you are making, and to consciously blend together diachronic and synchronic approaches. Furthermore, it is a good idea to carefully analyse dance historical publications by scholars whom you admire, in order to develop your understanding not just of what they are writing, but how they have carried out the research itself, the process and research methodology. This will probably mean re-reading texts, not for meaning this time, but for an insight into how the research itself has been built.

 Focus points

Key search terms: historiography, historical narrative, documentation, archive, archival and documenting practice, vernacular and social dance, diachronic, synchronic, teleology

Organisations: Society of Dance History Scholars, Society for Dance Research

Methodologies: historiography, performance, narrative and historiographic analysis, archival practice, ethnography

Philosophical approaches and ideology: cultural theory, modernism/postmodernism, identity politics, feminism, postcolonialism, phenomenology

Publications:

Carter, A. (ed.) (2004) *Rethinking Dance History: A Reader*. London: Routledge.

Dils, A. and Cooper Albright, A. (eds.) (2001) *Moving History/Dancing Cultures: A Dance History Reader*. Middletown, CT: Wesleyan University Press.

Kassing, G. (2007) *History of Dance: An Interactive Arts Approach*. Champaign, IL: Human Kinetics.

Adshead-Lansdale, J. and Layson. J. (1994) *Dance History: An Introduction*. 2nd edn, London: Routledge.

Foster, S.L. (ed.) (1996) *Corporealities: Dancing Knowledge, Culture and Power*. London: Routledge.

Teaching and learning

Researching a particular aspect of teaching and learning in dance can be a fruitful endeavour for your dissertation, particularly if you are interested in pursuing a career in secondary or primary education or other forms of teaching in dance. Pedagogy is the scholarly discipline that describes the theory and practice of education. It is linked with the term andragogy, which applies to the theory and practice of adult teaching and learning.

In the UK, the Post Graduate Certificate in Education (PGCE) is the generally accepted formal route into the teaching profession, whilst in the United States there is a more complex graduate system that varies dependent on state. Routes into formal teaching careers in other parts of the world may vary. It is important to check the routes open to you depending on where you wish to teach. It is understood that places for the more formal routes into teaching are competitive and a good degree outcome is necessary. In that respect, focusing on teaching and learning in your dissertation might be a productive introduction if you intend to take this career path. Teaching and learning can also include other contexts such as dance schools, companies and community practice. Less formal teaching might apply to community environments and more specialised contexts that focus on specific learning needs or on roles such as facilitator or instructor, perhaps in a health and leisure context.

In researching teaching and learning in dance, the focus is generally on practice and addresses the various approaches to teaching dance or movement and the particular learning styles that exist. The learning can be child-, student- and adult-focused and can cross over into developmental and dance psychology through an interest in motor function, cognition and motivational and other strategies for approaching dance-related issues. Dance teaching and learning often focuses on experiential acquisition of tacit knowledge through practice. Whilst technical ability in particular dance techniques might be well defined in terms of assessment, the way in which students will embody technique through learning and teaching is complex. Classes are often focused on observing, mirroring and responding to feedback given by the teacher.

It might be that you arrange to observe the teaching practices of professionals and compare approaches with advice from your dissertation tutor. You might decide to look at assessment and the ways of measuring particular learning outcomes. You might also choose to develop an inquiry around learning techniques, such as reflection and critique. You could look in more detail at methods and models of teaching, such as David Kolb's Learning Styles Model and/or Experiential Learning Theory (Kolb 2014). Care should be taken in forward planning if you wish to involve professionals, schools or organisations in your work and ethical considerations should be considered where necessary (check with your tutor).

 Focus points

Key search terms: pedagogy, andragogy, knowledge, skills, intelligence, learning style, teaching, instruction, learner motivation, reflexive practice, reflection, process-orientation, flow, experiential learning

Organisations: International Dance Teaching Association and National Dance Teaching Association (IDTA/NDTA), National Association of Teachers of Dancing (NATD), Imperial Society of Teachers of Dancing (ISTD), DanceHE, Royal Academy of Dance (RAD), bbodance

Methodologies: action research, grounded theory, ethnography

Philosophical approaches and ideology: pedagogy, andragogy, psychology, phenomenology

Publications:

> Pugh McCutchen, B. (2006) *Teaching Dance as Art in Education*. Champaign, IL: Human Kinetics.
> Smith-Autard, J.M. (2002) *The Art of Dance in Education*. London: A&C Black Publishers.
> Gibbons, E. (2007) *Teaching Dance: The Spectrum of Styles*. Bloomington, IN: AuthorHouse.
> Kolb, D.A. (2014) *Experiential Learning: Experience as the Source of Learning and Development*. 2nd edn, New Jersey: Pearson FT Press.

Community practice

Community dance is not easy to define, but it is largely agreed that the term refers to opportunities to participate in dance that are accessible to all. Community dance does not refer to a specific genre or style of dance, and encompasses a wide range of contexts, including working with young people at risk, older people, people with disabilities and those who are socially disadvantaged. Community dance practitioners tend to be committed to a set of shared values, including aiming to create positive experiences for people in, with and through dance, valuing diversity and practising inclusion.

If you are interested in pursuing community dance practice as a career, you may decide to use the dissertation project as an opportunity to develop your knowledge of a certain aspect of it. There is an emerging body of literature on community dance, advocated by organisations such as People Dancing – the Foundation for Community Dance, and Ausdance. It is a good idea to read broadly on the topic of community dance and get a sense of its historical development in your part of the world and beyond, by researching the people, organisations, institutions and political factors that have shaped its approaches. This could include government policies and funding arrangements that are intended to support community dance. It may be useful to expand your research beyond dance into the field of applied theatre, as there is a growing body of literature on this topic and many of the concepts and debates can usefully influence discussions on community dance.

In addition, you might gain access to dance in the community by leading, assisting with or observing sessions in order to develop your skills and insights about community dance in a specific context. You can find out about opportunities to connect with local community dance groups through your council's website. It can help to have a personal connection when approaching the dance group's leader to ask for permission to join in the sessions, observe and interview the participants, if appropriate. If not, it may still be possible to interview the person leading the group. If you are working directly with other people for your research, particularly vulnerable people, you will need to carefully consider research ethics, as introduced in Chapter 2.

It will be necessary to narrow down your research focus on a particular aspect of community dance: a specific local context, work with a particular age range or for a specific purpose. Possible themes that you might be interested in exploring in your dissertation could include dance and health, policies to make dance accessible for all, building a sense of community in urban areas, and community dance work to address social injustice and exclusion. Much community work is concerned with youth dance in various ways, such as project-based work or performance groups. A growing area of community dance practice is working with older people, raising questions about social perceptions of age and the ageing body. There may be some cross- or inter-generational practices local to you that you are interested in exploring. Established dance companies or cultural venues tend to undertake outreach work to engage the wider community with the art form.

Depending on the focus of your research, you will need to gain a thorough understanding of the circumstances and issues surrounding the selected practice, in order to deal with them sensitively and in a balanced way in your discussion. Therefore, it will be necessary to read more broadly about culture, identity and religious, social, psychological or medical issues as relevant. Your investigation could explore how community dance practitioners engage with people with respect for differences and create dance experiences that develop the participants' sense of self-worth, confidence and wellbeing.

In practical terms, you might develop your understanding of established approaches to leading workshops, as well as newer, emerging or more experimental ways of working.

- How and why are the specific methods for workshop facilitation used?
- What experiences do the activities create for the participants?
- Do choreography and performance play a role, and if so, how?
- Who attends the performance and how does dance touch the lives of others in the community in that way?
- How might we read the meanings that are constructed through those performances?

By studying the practical ways of working in community dance, your dissertation can create an interesting argument about how dance and its attention to the body can make a positive impact on these particular people's lives.

 Focus points

Key search terms: community, collaboration, social inclusion, diversity, accessibility, identity, difference, culture, equality, wellbeing, applied theatre

Organisations: People Dancing – Foundation for Community Dance, Ausdance

Methodologies: action research, ethnography, auto-ethnography, phenomenology

Philosophical approaches and ideology: cultural and identity theory, theory surrounding the body and agency, defining community practices and ideology

Publications:

> Amans, D. (ed.) (2008) *An Introduction to Community Dance Practice*. Basingstoke: Palgrave Macmillan.
> Hamera, J. (2006) *Dancing Communities: Performance, Difference and Connection in the Global City*. Basingstoke: Palgrave Macmillan.
> Kuppers, P. (2007) *Community Performance: An Introduction*. London: Routledge.
> Cooper Albright, A. (1997) *Choreographing Difference: The Body and Identity in Contemporary Dance*. Hanover, NH: Wesleyan University Press.

Media and technology

Researching media and technology in dance and performance practices can be a real opportunity to focus your skills in a specialist area that could lead to the development of an interdisciplinary or hybrid dance practice, or if you might find that you wish to alter your career path into more media-related industries.

The development of media and technology over the last fifty years has seen significant changes from analogue to digital practice. This has transformed the ways in which bodies interact and are represented through the use of different media and technologies. Dance and other performance disciplines have developed an interest in and engagement with the use of different types of media as tools for practice, research and performance. These media can be, but are not limited to, the World Wide Web, software and computer technology, film and photography, portable, locative and communications technology, robotics and biotechnology.

Dance research has focused on the role of media and technology in dance practice, teaching and learning, documentation and performance. In practice, digital tools have been created for the generation and development of movement, and dance can be emphasised or expressed through a variety of media forms. Both current and more dated (sometimes termed retro) media have been used to explore representation and themes in live performance works. Film and television have expanded the viewing platforms for dance and performance. Documentation in dance has revolved around recording and archiving performance and technique, so that they may be studied, taught, passed on and re-staged or re-worked. Specialities particular to dance on screen have led to forms such as 'Dance for Camera', 'Screendance' and more recent explorations in documentary practice. More recently technology is concerned with immersion and interactivity, which has interesting implications for performance.

Dance media and technology as a research area has always been concerned with the relationship between the machine and the body. This is particularly so since social and cultural attitudes have adapted to incorporate screen and communication devices as part of everyday lives. As such, dance is concerned with the implications of this on the notion of the 'lived' and 'dancing' body. Questions arise concerning what it now means to be human, embodied and 'real' and around the loss of bodily engagement we once relied upon when we were without particular technologies. Research questions can be explored through practice in innovative ways, involving blogging, online journaling, software/app development and practical engagement, filming and documenting practice.

 Focus points

Key search terms: mediation, medium as message, intermediality, liveness, presence, screen, representation, re-mediation, mediatised body, hybridity, cyborg, documenting practices, screendance, dance on screen, posthuman, mise-en-shot

Organisations: Dance Digital, The Centre For Screendance (University of Brighton)

Methodologies: screen-based performance analysis, archival research, phenomenology, ethnography, netnography, historiography

Philosophical approaches and ideology: communication theory and determinism, cultural theory, posthumanism, identity, phenomenology, theories surrounding the body and technology

Publications:

Blanco Borelli, M. (ed.) (2014) *The Oxford Handbook of Dance and the Popular Screen.* Oxford: Oxford University Press.

Broadhurst, S. and Machon, J. (2006) *Performance and Technology: Practices of Virtual Embodiment and Interactivity.* Basingstoke: Palgrave Macmillan.

Kozel, S. (2007) *Closer: Performance, Technologies, Phenomenology.* Cambridge, MA: MIT Press.

McPherson, K. (2006) *Making Video Dance.* London: Routledge.

Enterprise and business

Within this area, dance can be explored through its application in commercial settings. This encompasses the creative industries through the production, marketing, staging and performance of dance. It can also include a more entrepreneurial engagement in the business sector involving education, regional and local agencies, fitness and the specialist integration of dance practice within a business environment. The latter might inform and mirror particular concepts, principles and roles.

Researching these settings can include the cultural, political and financial implications surrounding dance and its production. Products in the dance industry can
include, but are not limited to, performances, workshops, teaching, clothing and
other merchandise, along with media and marketing. Dance as a business will
incorporate roles such as management, administration, production, curation, artistic
direction, media and marketing, as well as the more common dance roles of dancer,
choreographer, dance artist and agent.

Focusing on a career in dance in these commercial settings requires knowledge of
the different routes into dance and how dance is applied in a specific setting. Each
individual role has a particular part to play in promoting dance. Understanding
the necessary skills involved in this promotion is important. If chosen as a research
interest, it could open up a range of possibilities and opportunities to pursue in
your career.

Particular to business and enterprise are specific strategies and models of business practice that claim to lead to success or are selected to best fit the product or
service being marketed. Organisations are structured in different ways and tend to
follow identified practices of operation through various policies and procedures.
Of interest in these ways of working are issues of power, agency and control, along
with ethical responsibility and commercial gain.

From the dance artist through to international business, concerns surround sustainability, economic growth and developing the service or product you have for
your target market. Other questions might be more creatively generated around
choreographies within a workforce and the compositional techniques of a business
strategy, to think how dance could be metaphorically engaged within research in
this area. Again, you may choose to research this area through shadowing professionals, looking specifically at ways of working, policy and procedure or at proposed
developments and their impact on the business, individual or organisation.

Focus points

Key search terms: culture, commercialism, enterprise, economy, business administration,
dance production, profit, sustainability, ethical business practice, co-operatives, product development, dance marketing, dance roles, dance company administration, equality,
diversity

Organisations: Dance infrastructure agencies, e.g. Dance 4, Arts Council England

Methodologies: business and product analysis, action research, phenomenology,
ethnography

Philosophical approaches and ideology: economics, identity and political theories involving
capitalist/Marxist perspectives, business models and theories, organisational structures

Publications:

Hopgood, J. (2016) *Dance Production: Design and Technology*. New York: Focal Press.
Padgett, A.D. (2010) *How to Set Up a Successful Dance Class in 6 Easy Steps*. Dancing
  Detectives.
Cooper, S. (2007) *Staging Dance*. London: Routledge.

Science, health and wellbeing

Dance science and health is a very broad area that reflects interests in scientific performance research, along with current thinking around the promotion of wellbeing in and through dance practice. These appear to be at opposing ends of a spectrum and can be seen as distinctly separate approaches to the body. It could be said that the former does favour a more experimental approach to methodology, whilst the latter could favour more qualitative and interpretive approaches to research.

Dance science as an area seeks to promote practices, research, strategies and knowledge to optimise performance in dancers and pays particular attention to anatomy, physiology and kinesiology. These specialisms allow for the study of the moving body and body systems in addressing safe dance practice, injury and rehabilitation, conditioning and nutrition. Former research exists as a bank of resources, through which particular protocols and models of working and testing can assist researchers with specific inquiries around the area of dance practice and performance. Whilst research will often involve volunteer participants, it might be extended to testing equipment, treatments, techniques and nutritional products. You might be engaged in strategies for keeping the dancing body in peak condition, looking at specific injuries and their management. You could also investigate product design and development.

Dance psychology can be seen to come from sports psychology, which tends to be focused on achievement and goal orientation in relation to improving performance, stamina and quality. It can also be focused on holistic and humanist perspectives, addressing individual patterns of being and responding that directly impact on our posture, attitudes, beliefs and general physicality.

Dance and wellbeing can be seen to incorporate practices and concerns that promote holistic approaches to the maintenance and care of both dancers and non-dancers, depending on the setting. Incorporated in this are therapeutic practices that involve Dance Movement Therapy (DMT) or Dance Movement Psychotherapy (DMP), where qualified practitioners work in a variety of settings from community or lone working to working for and with organisations and in public settings.

Somatic practice is an umbrella term for a range of movement practices that denote a fundamental focus on connecting mind and body. These practices, such as yoga, Body-Mind Centering and Pilates to name a few, are often forms of body conditioning that dancers engage with to ground themselves in their dance practice. They are also practised by non-dancers to feel more centred in life. Instructors in these techniques should have a recognised qualification and may hold classes independently or practice within an organisational setting. Research might involve reflection on particular practices over time through analysis and ethnographic approaches, shadowing professionals with the relevant ethics approval and a focus on personal practice and experiential research.

These areas of dance science, health and wellbeing provide a rich platform for research and reflect concerns surrounding the self-care and health of the dancer/dance artist, as well as a more general appreciation of the social and cultural understanding of wellbeing.

Focus points

Key search terms: exercise conditioning, injury prevention and rehabilitation, healthy dancer, somatics, performance psychology, optimisation and periodisation, health, fitness, wellbeing, flexibility, biomechanics, physiology, podiatry, nutrition, corporeality, humanist psychology, holism

Organisations: One Dance UK, International Association for Dance Medicine and Science (IADMS), National Institute of Dance Medicine and Science (NIDMS)

Methodologies: experimental research (including design), action research, phenomenology, ethnography

Philosophical approaches and ideology: physiology, biomechanics, positivism and post-positivism, anti-Cartesian perspectives, somatics, holism, psychology, identity, cultural theory

Publications:

> Berg, K.E. and Latin, R.W. (2008) *Essentials of Research Methods in Health, Physical Education, Exercise Science, and Recreation.* 3rd edn, Baltimore, MD: Lippincott Williams & Wilkins.
>
> Quin, E., Rafferty, S. and Tomlinson, C. (2015) *Safe Dance Practice: An Applied Dance Science Perspective.* Champaign, IL: Human Kinetics.
>
> Whatley, S., Garrett Brown, N. & Alexander, K. (2015) *Attending to Movement: Somatic Perspectives on Living in This World.* Axminster: Triarchy Press.

Activity: Navigating the clusters of interest

Identify which cluster or clusters of interest is/are most relevant for your topic area.

Explore in depth the focus points attached to the cluster through your own independent research. Use as much of the resources available to you to conduct your research (library, online journal databases). Make sure to schedule plenty of time to achieve comprehensive and in-depth engagement with the cluster.

What are the key research methods, concepts, theories and perspectives that you encounter in that cluster that are connected to your inquiry?

As you go along, complete the following by selecting relevant elements informed by the cluster of interest that aligns with your topic:

> Research aim:
> Methods:
> Theories:
> Methodology:
> Concepts:
> Perspectives/voices:
> Resources/access:

Student comments:

'How did you research?'

'I read specific articles about the historical development of my subject area to gain an idea of its context. I highlighted ways in which I could link this development to present day.'

'To understand more about the area, I researched on Google Scholar and Google Books initially. From this search, I identified the most useful books and ordered them. I also downloaded journal articles that were relevant to my topic. From this, I collated the information, drew up mind maps of different related terms and then chose the path I wanted to follow.'

'I read books and journals. Important quotes were highlighted and referenced as starting points to discuss ideas.'

'I wanted to do my dissertation on physiology, so I looked at the different aspects of physiology and the ways in which these could be linked to dance. This included reading text books about physiology to understand how this discipline could apply to dance. I read about studies that had already been done in dance and sports and used the bibliographies at the end of these articles to find more relevant sources for research.'

Summary points:

Your research methodology combines all the research methods you have used and the theoretical framework that has shaped your thinking. It is important to be aware of your methodology and articulate it explicitly in your dissertation.

Your methodology and particular ways of thinking may be strongly influenced by a particular research philosophy. Again, it is useful to bring this to the fore in your dissertation to show your awareness of the field.

Reviewing the established methodologies and clusters of interest outlined in this chapter will help you to identify what your research is aligned with and where it fits in. This process will entail a thorough, independent engagement with the key search terms, debates, methodologies, philosophical approaches and publications that characterise that part of the field.

Ensuring that your research is connected to and builds on the work of other researchers in your area will make your dissertation more relevant, valid and persuasive.

Chapter 4
Outward facing: presenting and communicating the research

Imagine you are a craftsman, who is busy creating an object. It could be a decorative piece of woodcraft, a piece of pottery or a piece of lace textile. You are using your hands and your fine motor skills to carefully shape the object, so that it will stand out to its users as a perfect combination of form and function. The concept of the artefact is clear to its users and has a certain simplicity about it. Nevertheless, it is intricate and refined where necessary, without overwhelming the user of the object with too much detail.

Beyond the heavy toil of the dissertation research work discussed in Chapter 3, where you are considering and employing a range of research methods and engaging with various theoretical perspectives, the work is far from over. This chapter will guide you through the more intricate and refined work, or crafting, of your research findings as you communicate them to readers and audiences. This will entail you finding your voice as a writer, scholar and/or artist, and growing more confident in how you deliver your message.

In the introduction to this book, we referred to the sometimes uneasy relationship that exists between dance as an embodied practice and written communication. Translating our experience of dance into words is challenging and inevitably flawed; yet there is tremendous value in attempting to communicate about dance through language. It can help you to reach new audiences for your ideas and open doors to new networks, opportunities and partnerships. A strong command of language can enable you to access funding and be an advocate for dance. Being able to write well is also a general asset for careers in other fields. The dissertation offers you an extended learning opportunity to develop your communication and persuasion skills, in order for you to reach your professional aims.

Nevertheless, it is also worth continuing to monitor and acknowledge the limitations of dance writing. In your project, you can keep open a space for ambiguity and a multitude of experiences, by employing a tentative, reflective or creative writing style when needed. This will be explored in one of the subsections of this chapter.

Important questions to ask yourself include:

- How can I communicate effectively my insights from research?
- What is the most suitable output and communication mode for my subject matter? How might practice say something? What is the language of practice?
- How can I bridge the divide between non-verbal dance experience and language? Why should I try?
- How can I take ownership of a large document and structure it creatively?
- How can I convince the reader of my argument?
- What writing style(s) might I employ, when and for what purpose?
- How can I engage audiences in an oral presentation?
- How will I persuade assessors of the strengths of my research in a viva voce?

In this chapter, the emphasis will be placed on communicating the research outwards through writing or sharing the research via other outputs and modes of communication.

Modes of presentation

This section introduces and explores the different modes you might consider to present your research outcomes. It goes without saying that you must fit your work into one of the assessment formats prescribed in the briefing document of your degree course. However, higher education courses are increasingly making use of 'negotiated assessment' in order to actively involve students in designing their own assessment formats to suit their personal learning aims and projects. Even if the assessment briefing document is prescriptive, it should still be possible for you to find room for creativity to adapt the output to best accommodate the needs of your project. Negotiating the mode of output for your dissertation can be done at the proposal stage or it can become part of the conversations you have with your tutor at a later stage.

 Focus points

You are encouraged to make conscious decisions about the research output you will use for your dissertation research by carefully considering a range of possibilities:

- writing
- performances
- films
- presentations
- lecture demonstrations
- visual elements
- web-based platforms
- any combination of the above.

You can creatively mobilise one or more of the above possibilities to communicate your research findings in a valid and rigorous way.

When deciding your research output, it is a good idea to focus on the opportunities and risks that are inherent in each mode.

You should carefully consider the particular challenges of practice-based work:

- documentation of your work and process
- access to performers
- access to rehearsal space
- access to filming equipment and editing software.

Plan forward to meet these challenges head on so that they do not hinder your progress.

Practice-based research outputs

If you have the opportunity for practice outcomes, possible choices of the kind of practice you may present could include performance, demonstration, workshop, film and documentary, but are not limited to these. When making your choice, you should consider how you might creatively and effectively put across key elements of your research inquiry and findings through the practice form. You should also consider what is possible within the time constraints that you have.

Sometimes pieces of practice developed for research projects may reference a theme with only surface depth initially. This does not adequately or creatively evidence a critical inquiry yet. Critical approaches to practice should evidence how you have questioned or explored your chosen themes and made choices of what to include.

- What will be highlighted or made clear through the practice?
- Why is this form of practice the best option as an outcome of this research?

When undertaking practice-based research, form and content are fundamental considerations. These should be developed within the context of your practice and be clearly evident in the final output of your research project. Practice work can demonstrate research findings, research concepts and/or research inquiries. It can also be the research itself as well as be about the research, i.e. an aspect of technique, a new approach to practice, or a method. The work needs to be inquiry-based, stemming from a place of exploration, questioning, experimentation and reflection. Other linked terms to read around in this area are practice-led research and practice-as-research (PaR).

Documentation

Often, documentation is a requirement for practice-based research outcomes. The need to be selective about what material is documentation and what is practice is important here. Documentation is usually identified as a creative representation of the work carried out through the process and the approaches used to arrive at the outcome. In this way, it is not the work itself that is documented. Instead, you as researcher will step back to reflect on the process that resulted in the practice you presented. The best way to do this accurately is to consider documentation as a part of your methodology, i.e. something documented as a continued process. Dancers are used to keeping creative journals and it is much the same. You might reflect using process notes that can be represented through an online blog or website. They might be represented visually through photography or film, or recorded sound as a podcast. You could produce a map, diagram or illustration or use artefacts and weave a narrative of the work around them. You need to consider what resources in terms of space, materials, technical assistance and equipment are available to you and how you might best use them to document the research process.

Focus points

In my practice-based research, I wanted to explore the topic of performance anxiety. I decided to invite participant dancers to workshops incorporating task-based activities around their experiences of performance anxiety. I sought the relevant permissions by submitting an ethics form and creating participant information sheets. The tasks were recorded in my process journal and I used both photography and film to capture the material from the tasks set for participants.

These task-based activities resulted in written poetry, movement material and spoken word. In the next stage of my research, I reflected on this material and what it contributed to an understanding of performance anxiety. I used my process journal to evaluate the key insights emerging from both the process and the material gathered. Using formerly researched theories and concepts, I critically reflected on these insights gathered to high-light any new understandings.

Following this, I invited the same dancers to further explore significant material from the tasks in a choreographic process that further developed the research findings.

Overall, in making decisions about your research output and mode of presentation, you may want to consider your own learning preferences and learning needs. How do you want to strengthen, challenge and expand your individual skill set? Some students actively use the dissertation to work on their writing skills. Others use it as an opportunity to practice their public speaking skills through a lecture demonstration. Others proactively aim to develop their choreographic skills and their voice as an emerging dance artist. You can explore these questions through your own reflective practice, by discussing them with a fellow student or by seeking advice from a tutor.

Activity: Matching your research output to your learning goals

Explore and evaluate a range of possible modes of presentation and research outputs, reflecting on your learning preferences, learning needs and professional career ideas.

- What will best meet the needs of your inquiry?
- What output will make use of your existing skills and strengths?
- How can your research output push you to develop other skills that you need or want to work on?
- What research output will be most useful for your potential future career?
- How might your research output create career opportunities?

Then, if relevant and necessary, discuss with your tutor your research output choices.

Structuring a large document creatively

The dissertation (typically 7,000–10,000 words in length, although institutional requirements may vary) may be the largest text that you have set out to write in your (academic) career so far. You may be feeling challenged by the prospect of managing a document of this size. By making use of the anchor points in your support network – your tutor, your peers, your own reflective research and writing practice – you will be able to conquer this challenge. The sense of achievement you will derive from completing a substantial dissertation should fill you with confidence to tackle large projects in the future. Therefore, this section will help you to think strategically and creatively about how you might structure your dissertation text, so that you can keep on top of the complexity of the material and work towards completing the text.

The guidance in this book is intended to be used as a support alongside the guidance given by your university or college, and any specific briefing documents outlining the requirements of your specific institution. Nevertheless, we would encourage you to find room for creativity within the guidelines to tailor the presentation of your research findings to the particular aims of your project. This is part of finding your own voice as a scholar, artist and/or emerging professional. If you approach the negotiation of individual variants to the presentation of your research in a clear, well-reasoned and professional manner, your tutors and institution may well be open and supportive of your proposal.

Some general dissertation study guides, or those focused on the social sciences, tend to prescribe a set structure for the dissertation. Often, these are modelled on the research practices of the social sciences. These guides provide a set order of sections that your dissertation should include: literature review, methods, findings and results, and discussion. While it can be comforting to rely on such a seemingly methodical way of structuring your text, research in dance is conducted by its own, often interdisciplinary, methods. Moreover, adopting a borrowed set structure from another academic discipline for your dance dissertation can have the undesired effect of making your research come across as pseudo-scientific. It affords the work a scientific air, but the prescribed sections of the dissertation do not add any real value to your work as a piece of dance research. Instead, they use up precious words, which you could have used more effectively in a more integrated way by coming up with your own structure.

Most of all, it would befit the creativity of the artistic practices and dancing bodies that you are studying to respond in your dissertation with an equally creative structure that is carefully attuned to the particular needs of your research project. Of course, connecting to the field, research methods and theoretical frameworks, discussed in previous chapters, should all be addressed within the dissertation text, but the discussion of these elements need not simply be located exactly in a prescribed section. Instead, they may be woven into your writing throughout the document when relevant. When engaging with published dance research, you might find many salient examples of dance scholars who have interwoven reference to literature with analysis and discussion, all rolled into a single section. Description of research methods can be done in just a few sentences, as there are perhaps fewer factual parameters to consider compared to the social sciences.

Overall, you will need to decide on the number and content of chapters/sections you will need, weigh up chapter length versus depth and think about how the chapters speak to one another in the context of the entire dissertation. Making decisions of this kind about your dissertation structure requires high-level, advanced communication skills. Therefore, you are encouraged to meet this challenge head on as an opportunity to learn and practise these advanced skills to the maximum. Later on in the writing process, it may become clear that your initial structure will need to be revised. A chapter may need to be split into two, or a particular section may need to be moved from one chapter to another. There may be a need to add a new chapter altogether, or it may become clear that there is not enough scope or room in the dissertation for one of the chapters that you had originally envisaged. You will need to respond to these thoughts bravely and with the agility and flexibility that we practise in our dancing lives.

Critical mass?

'Critical mass' may be a helpful metaphor to consider in this context. You could think about critical mass as a stage in the development of the material at which it can withstand questioning and still hold up as a convincing piece of work that the author can get behind. The work needs to demonstrate that the author has a thorough knowledge of the field and that the ideas put forward in the dissertation are not isolated, but connected to other significant voices in the field. The work needs to lay out a convincing collection of evidence in order to support the arguments that are developed in the text. There should be an awareness and acknowledgement of possible counter-arguments, and the author should recognise a degree of ambiguity and uncertainty in the argument. In short, in order to decide whether your work achieves sufficient critical mass, you will need to assess whether you have presented material of sufficient sophistication and complexity for the reader.

 Focus points

Questions that may help you decide on a structure for your dissertation text could include:

- How many words (estimate) should each section or chapter contain for it to achieve 'critical mass'? Chapters of fewer than 1,000 words are unlikely to enable you to put forward a level of thinking that is sufficiently in-depth and complex.
- How many key ideas do you think are vital to expand and elaborate for the reader? Can there be such a thing as too many avenues explored in the dissertation? If so, how do you decide where to direct the reader's focus? Usually, it is advisable to unpack no more than three or four aspects of your dissertation topic within in-depth chapters.
- What kinds of connection to the field do you plan to make in each chapter or section? Which aspects of literature research would you bring in to which chapter? Which central concepts will shape your approach in each chapter?
- What dance or performance examples, or case studies, will you analyse in which chapter or section?

- What other evidence (interview material, archival research, discourse analysis, and so on) can you bring in to which chapter to strengthen your case?
- How might readers critically respond to your arguments? What counterarguments or critical questions might they raise in response? Would addressing these enhance and strengthen your work or not?

Answering these questions through your own reflective practice can help you to make the necessary strategic decisions about the dissertation's structure and chapter length. Your tutor and your peers tend to make good reflective dialogue partners. They can act as a useful sounding board, as you determine your dissertation structure.

It is reasonable that the structure of the dissertation will evolve through an iterative process of moulding and re-moulding, refining and enhancing the structure through subtle or sometimes quite radical shifts. You may need a visual mapping system to represent the various ideas, case studies and connections between them. Some students prefer to draw up a spider diagram; others use coloured sticky notes to enable them to literally move ideas from one part of the room to another. You will need to adopt an attitude of resilience to cope effectively, imaginatively and productively with this kind of conceptual restructuring. Students who have restructured their dissertation during the research process report that, although it was difficult to make the decision and then deal successfully with the implications of the change, their dissertation became much stronger once they had done it. You are the author of the document, and therefore it is important to remain in control of it and not let the dissertation be in control of you.

Activity: Coming up with a structure for your dissertation
- Before you commit to a linear structure, carry out a visual mapping of the ideas and case studies that will form part of your dissertation research.
- Create a spider diagram or use coloured sticky notes to group ideas together into clusters.
- Then, move the ideas into a linear form, thinking about an order for the material that creates through-lines of connection in the inquiry.
- Use that as a basis for discussion with your peers and tutor.

Introduction

The introduction is arguably one of the most important sections of the dissertation. It eases the reader into your research project, delineating its scope and parameters, and clarifying its approach, methods and research questions. A good introduction offers the reader an opportunity to mentally prepare for what is to come. By writing a clear and informative introduction, you can fill the reader with confidence that you have carefully considered the necessary issues and aspects of the research topics, and you can pre-emptively alleviate possible concerns and questions the reader might have prior to engaging with the main body of the dissertation.

Some students prefer to wait until the end of the writing process to write the introduction. It is worth considering doing this, because it will be easier to write a good introduction informed by reflection on the research project as a whole and the decisions you made along the way. If you prefer to begin by writing the introduction at the start of the process, it is strongly recommended that you revisit it at the end of the process anyway, to ensure that it accurately reflects the shape that the project has taken through time.

A key job of the introduction is to carve out a space for your research:

- Provide a brief outline of the research topic, explaining what it is exactly that your dissertation focuses on.
- Situate your research in relation to a specific area or combination of areas of the field, in order to clarify how your research will connect to and build on established research in the field.
- Introduce the research questions and make a case for the reasons why it is relevant or important to ask them.
- Explain your research methodology; in other words which research methods or activities you have used as a researcher, and which theoretical perspectives and concepts you are drawing on in your analysis and discussion.
- Outline the aims of the research, so that the reader is clear on what you have set out to do in your project; this is referred to as a thesis statement.
- Guide the reader through the large document that is to follow. Explain how the dissertation is structured and what each chapter aims to achieve. Including an organisational statement like this provides the necessary signposting to guide the reading process.

Formulating a **thesis statement** is not easy. It requires extraordinary language and communication skills to capture the essence of the research project in an engaging, yet concise manner. A tip you might like to try out throughout the research process is to regularly revisit you key statement, which outlines the aims of your research, every day that you work on the dissertation. With each day that passes, your thinking about the project will develop, change and slightly shift. Perhaps you only need to tweak a few words in your statement; perhaps you need to wipe the slate clean and start again from scratch. Committing to a regular act of rephrasing your research aims will enable you to continuously refine your statement, and constitutes a useful part of reflective practice in the research process.

Conclusion

Another important section of your dissertation is the conclusion. The conclusion is a final opportunity to reinforce the key points of your research findings and argument to the reader.

- Revisit the aims and reasons for the research.
- Summarise the accomplishments and argument of each chapter. However, the conclusion should do more than simply reiterate the points already made; instead, it should look for wider, underlying insights connecting the ideas of the different chapters together.

- Build further connections to the wider field and open up avenues for further research.
- Review the effectiveness of the research methodology that you used in the dissertation (see below for further guidance).

Although the different chapters of the main body of the dissertation might be read in isolation as mini-essays, the dissertation as a whole is greater than the sum of its parts. By reading the dissertation as a whole, culminating in a substantial conclusion, the reader will glean new, wider insights that may not have emerged had the dissertation not been put together in that way.

Many students find conclusions hard to write. It can feel as if you are repeating the same points that you have already made previously in the individual chapters. However, by finding new ways of rephrasing the same insights, you will clarify the points already made, shed new light on your research findings and illuminate certain connections. Moreover, in the conclusion, you are looking to establish wider observations and more general thoughts about the research topic, by focusing on what connects the insights in the different chapters together.

Contrary to the advice given about when to write the introduction, and perhaps counter-intuitively, you might try to write a preliminary conclusion at the start of the research process. Articulating what you expect to find out through your research can help to kick-start your thinking. Of course, you will revisit the conclusion at the end of the research and writing process, and reflect on whether your initial thoughts match your final reflections or not, and why that might be the case. Perhaps you will find a way to weave those thoughts into your conclusion itself.

Finally, another function of the conclusion is to review the effectiveness of the research methodology that you used in the dissertation. This goes further than stating whether or not it was effective, particularly because you are expected to adapt and adjust your methodology throughout the project through a process of reflective practice. Nevertheless, it is useful to share with the reader what the particular benefits were of a certain research method, theoretical perspective or concept. Likewise, it can show an even higher level of academic maturity if you are able to articulate the limitations of the methodological decisions that you made. However, the conclusion is not the time to self-deprecate; instead, you need to find a way of highlighting any potential limitations in your work without devaluing the accomplishments of your project.

Abstract

An abstract is a very brief text at the start of a research output, usually no longer than 250–300 words. Scholarly journal articles and conference papers tend to be preceded by an abstract. The purpose of this paragraph is to outline the scope of the research and summarise the argument so that the reader can decide whether or not to read the document in full. In other words, the abstract offers a little more depth about the nature of the research beyond what a reader can glean from the title. In some ways, it could be considered a 'sales pitch' for the research, which can help scholars increase the reach and impact of their work.

The abstract should read more like a conclusion than an introduction. The abstract should not state the aims of the research, but summarise its outcomes and achievements. It should not be written in the future tense, but in the present tense.

Of course, because undergraduate dissertations are not normally in the public domain, there is no immediate need for an abstract to inform and attract potential readers. Therefore, writing the abstract is a theoretical and hypothetical exercise for most students, without any real direct purpose. Therefore, it may be helpful to pause and think about why lecturers insist on making you do this exercise.

- What skills are you developing by writing this 250-word abstract for your dissertation or final year project?
- In what context do you anticipate having to use these skills in the future?

Constructing an argument

In order to persuade the reader of a particular point of view, you will need to construct an argument and provide supporting evidence to substantiate the claims you are making. Some students approach the dissertation as an assemblage of material, in other words, a gathering, reproduction and accumulation of information and ideas. However, the act of gathering alone is not enough to result in a successful dissertation. In order to create a meaningful research-based dissertation, you must be able to persuade the reader of your way of thinking about the topic. In contrast to what many students have taken away with them from secondary education, an argument is not simply the consideration of a number of points for and against a specific way of thinking. A scholarly, research-based argument aims to transform the reader's understanding of an issue.

An argument is different from a subjective opinion, because it is substantiated with evidence. Therefore, it is not advisable to use phrases such as 'in my opinion' in the dissertation; instead, ensure that you have persuaded the reader of your point of view with convincing evidence. What forms can evidence take in a research-based dissertation in dance?

- Evidence can exist in your analysis of the dance practice or discourse with which you are engaging.
- You might find evidence in an established theoretical concept, perspective or framework.
- Evidence can also lie in other authors' views or arguments, and can take the form of a citation or quotation.
- Outcomes and statistics gathered through surveys and questionnaires are yet another form of evidence.

Be guided by the established ways of working in the area of the field that you are focusing on, in order to avoid the use of evidence that may seem alien. It is not necessary to use all possible types of evidence in a single dissertation.

Focus point

You must ask yourself the following questions about each section of the dissertation, each chapter, each subsection, each paragraph and perhaps even each sentence.

* What is it that you want the reader to understand differently about this topic?
* What precise point are you trying to make?
* How will you persuade the reader of this argument?

Every chapter, section, paragraph and sentence must have a purpose for being there. As the author, you need to be clear of what that purpose is. If you are not clear about that, then who is?

This means that maybe you will need to make ruthless decisions to omit parts or sentences that distract from the argument you are trying to make.

Persuasive writing also means guiding the reader through complex information by exposing relationships and links between ideas and material. It is important to avoid the 'shopping list' approach, in which students merely cover ideas and accumulate material. Instead, really think about how one idea relates to the next. If there is no relationship, then why are these two sections together in the same chapter? If one idea really has no bearing on the other, then remove it. If there is a link, it is your job to bring that relationship to the surface for your reader through your writing.

When employing commonly used linking words, consider guarding against the over-use of the word 'however', which expresses a relationship of contradiction between what is to follow and what came before. If you have to use the word 'however' several times in one paragraph, it may be that the order of the sentences in your paragraph needs changing. Consider re-ordering the material so that you group together all material in support of a point and then group together all material that nuances and seemingly contradicts that point. Then, weigh up all the material in a concluding summary statement and clarify what you need the reader to understand from the section on balance.

Focus point

Many students, especially visual thinkers, struggle with the linearity of written academic arguments.

* You may need to colour-code your draft, marking sections or sentences addressing particular topics in different colours. If your text has become a patchwork of different colours, you should consider restructuring it.
* When you have assembled a substantial amount of research, it is useful to place yourself in the shoes of the reader by imagining you encounter the research material for the first time with fresh eyes.

- What does the reader need to know first, second and third, before moving on to another, more complex point?
- If this kind of ordering of information does not come naturally to you, you may need to experiment with reshuffling the material into a different order and reading it with fresh eyes to see how it flows.

Finally, to strengthen the argument you are making in your dissertation, it can be useful to demonstrate an awareness of your research methodology along the way. By rationalising and articulating explicitly how you have made specific decisions about the research (the 'why?' and 'how?'), you will be able to both demonstrate the depth of your understanding of the field and its methodological challenges, and guide the reader through the research. This kind of self-reflexive approach will demonstrate to the reader that you are aware of the constructed nature of research-based arguments.

Activity: Writing persuasively

Engage in reflective practice about your writing in response to the questions previously outlined in the focus point on critical mass. Hold a reflective conversation with your peers or tutor guided by these questions, or write a reflective response in your process journal. The outcomes of the reflective practice activity can be embedded in discussion in the dissertation.

Make a visual map of your dissertation text, tracing the through-line of your argument or inquiry. What is the argument, purpose and evidence underpinning each section, chapter or paragraph? This way you can see if each chapter and paragraph is clearly contributing to the points you are trying to communicate.

Be sure to trace each of the following elements:

- connections to the field, literature research, concepts/theories
- analysis of examples or case studies
- evidence.

Make decisions about the order and relevance of the different sections. Shift sections around if it would make the through-line clearer and stronger. Make sure that each chapter is connected to the field and includes sufficient analysis and evidence. Remove any unsubstantiated claims that are not backed up by evidence. Also remove any sections that don't add anything to your argument or inquiry.

Clarify the links between chapters and sections. Include signposting and signalling devices to guide the reader about what is to come and what has been covered so far.

Writing styles

By the time you write your final year dissertation, you are encouraged to use the writing apparatus strategically, with awareness and an ability to employ different writing styles, or registers, for specific purposes. Rather than providing fail-safe writing tips, this section provides a more considered approach which takes account of the full range of writing strategies embraced by the dance field.

Is it a good idea to avoid the use of the first person in academic writing, or could there be a case for bringing in your personal voice into your writing? There is no straightforward answer to this question. Consider the effect that the use of the word 'I' may have on the reader. Usually, it is better not to use the first person when writing in a scholarly, discursive style. However, there is a strong case for using 'I' in reflective writing.

Discursive writing

Discursive writing style is used to bring in other authors' arguments and insights into your own discussion. You will need to develop strategies to weave the voices of other scholars into your writing. This is important to demonstrate to the reader how you are connecting to the field, as explored in Chapter 1, and the need to acknowledge the ideas and material of others through referencing, described in Chapter 2.

There are two ways of bringing in someone else's idea into your own discussion:

- using a direct quotation

  or

- paraphrasing the author's material, which means rephrasing it in your own words.

The sources of both quotations and paraphrased material need to be acknowledged with a citation in the precise place in your text where they are included, in accordance with the referencing system your university or college requires you to use.

Quotations should be used sparingly, because if you use too many quotations, you run the risk that other scholars' voices overpower your own. Only use a direct quotation if, by changing the author's words, you would be altering their meaning. Perhaps there is a particular use of language that you wish to draw attention to. In all other cases it is better to paraphrase, the more challenging of the two options. Paraphrasing someone else's work can be exposing, because the reader will be able to see how you are interpreting the significance of the other author's insights. In some cases, the reader will be able to see how well you have understood the other author's work. Have you only understood the main points, or are you able to reflect the complexity of the author's thoughts in your writing? There may be gaps in your understanding or even misunderstandings that are revealed through your paraphrasing. As long as you do everything in your power to minimise these risks, it is far better to paraphrase. Paraphrasing is a skill that must be practised and will be incredibly useful in later life, in terms of connecting to what others are communicating.

Focus point

When bringing another scholar's voice into your own discussion, it is vital that you engage with it. It is not sufficient to simply drop an author's concept or argument into your discussion and leave it there. Instead:

- Clarify for the reader how and why this insight is relevant and important to your own analysis or to the development of your own argument.
- Identify not only the benefits of key perspectives, but also the limitations, and try to mitigate against these by defending your decision to use it after all.
- Establish links between one concept or perspective and another.
- Help the reader to see how the work of different scholars is connected, and where you situate your own research in relation to them.

Tentative or confident tone of writing?

You should carefully consider when it is necessary to adopt a tentative and careful tone of writing and when displaying confidence in the statements you are making is more effective. When you are not entirely sure about the truthfulness of a claim or insight, it is advisable to use words such as 'may', 'tends to', 'perhaps' or 'possible'. This is of particular importance when making general statements for which you are not going to take the space to back them up with evidence.

When making your own argument based on the research you have conducted and the evidence that you are presenting, it will be more effective to adopt a confident tone of writing. Confident writing means:

- using an active rather than passive voice
- using a direct rather than convoluted style
- using short and clear sentences.

The aim is to demonstrate confidence in the argument that you have constructed in order to persuade the reader of your way of thinking about this research topic and instruct them about what they need to know and understand about it. Particularly, statements that are specific and niche, about which you have in-depth knowledge and could be considered an expert at this stage, benefit from a direct and confident tone of writing.

Reflective writing

Dance writing is often based on careful personal reflections about the experience of performing or watching dance. You may have used reflective practice as a research method when considering your thoughts, feelings, insights and responses to a certain experience, and writing them down in a journal. There may be a strong case for including some of these reflections in your dissertation as evidence, if relevant to your inquiry. By bringing in your own personal, subjective voice, you would join a group of dance scholars in an exploration of phenomenology, which focuses on the lived experience, who use reflective writing to challenge positivist approaches to the creation of knowledge.

As with reflective practice in general, it is important to move your reflections beyond the merely descriptive and lift them up to a more advanced and sophisticated level to make them useful to your research process. While reflective writing is emerging in a range of areas of the dance field, it is not (yet) widely accepted practice. Therefore, if you decide to employ a reflective voice in your writing:

- Do so with a strong awareness, so that you do not give the reader any cause to doubt your approach.
- Be selective in the excerpts of reflective writing that you include in the dissertation.
- Clearly command the shifts in writing style between reflective and more conventionally scholarly sections.

Creative writing

Other creative approaches to writing for which a case could be made for inclusion in the dissertation might be based on, for example:

- poetry
- stories
- scripted dialogue
- word landscapes.

If you are interested in exploring the boundaries of what dance writing is and what it can do, you could experiment with creative tasks throughout your writing process. At a later stage you can then decide whether it would be useful to include some of those creative texts in the dissertation, if you think they would help you to convey your argument effectively. In some ways, it may be useful to think of your readers as an audience, for whom you might create a choreographic or theatrical experience of some sort, using all the textual tools at your disposal.

Activity: Learning about writing style from authors you admire

- Find an excerpt from a chapter or article by a dance writer whose writing you admire.
- Re-read the text, not simply for meaning and understanding, but to gain a sense of how the author uses language to convey a point.
- Analyse what is effective in the writer's approach and why.
- Can you, and would you want to, emulate that author's approach in your own writing?
- Try to find other examples and take the best approaches from different writers to create your own, unique writing style.

Programme notes for practice-based dissertation performances or presentations

If you are intending to present your practice-based research as a performance or presentation, you might consider producing a programme note or leaflet for the audience. While for lecture demonstrations an abstract and list of selected references would be useful, for a performance of choreographic work, you might consider taking a more creative and dramaturgical approach. Programme notes must include the necessary factual information and may include other artistic elements to guide the audience:

- the work's title
- the names of performers and collaborators
- music credits
- one or more images
- a brief text, perhaps a poem, story or word landscape.

A combination of the above can be a way to engage the audience with the experience and/or themes of your work. Be careful not to explain the work. Instead, try to open up unexpected avenues of thinking for the spectator, by revealing insights from the research or creative process, if appropriate, and by exploring creative writing.

Speaking about your research

Speaking about your research in a viva voce may be part of the dissertation assessment process in your university or college. Alternatively, you may be required to present your research findings in a conference-style, oral presentation. The reason why spoken communication in one of these forms is built into the process is that these learning opportunities offer students a chance to develop their skills in yet another mode of communication, which will be useful in professional life. Moreover, articulating your thoughts in spoken form may be helpful in giving your research more focus in its argumentation, either through a structured conversation or formal presentation (as in the speaking and listening exercise at the end of Chapter 1). Having people in the room, listening to you setting out key aspects of your research, may give you a valuable insight into how it is received by them; you might read people's body language and register any non-verbal communication to gain a sense of how convincing what you are saying is to them. With written communication, of course, you would not have a chance to gauge the immediate reaction of the reader.

Viva voce

The thought of a viva voce might be daunting to you. Officially, a viva voce is intended for you to defend your research in response to an examiner's interrogation, in order to see whether you have sufficient knowledge of the field to robustly answer probing questions. Another reason for a university or college to include a viva in the assessment process is to ascertain whether the student has produced the dissertation independently, to minimise the risk of academic misconduct in the form of 'ghost-writing'. While these institutional drivers are important in upholding the required academic standards, the pressure that is placed on students in this approach is considerable.

As a student, you might benefit from re-framing the viva in your mind in a different way; instead of thinking about it as a defence of your work under attack, it may help to think about it as a conversation between you and the assessor as peers, who both share an interest in the same field. You could think about the viva as an opportunity to engage in a meaningful conversation about your research with somebody who has taken the time to carefully read your work, and whose questions can help to push your thinking into even more interesting places. Although it is easier said than done, try to be confident about the work you have done in your dissertation.

 Focus point

Questions the assessor might ask you, for which you might prepare answers in advance, could include:

- What interested you about this research topic?
- How did you decide on your research focus?
- What is the main argument in your dissertation? Why is it important?
- Why was your chosen theoretical framework the most appropriate? Why did you not use [another theoretical concept]?
- How would you address the criticism that ... [potential weakness in your work]?
- If you could do the dissertation all over again, what would you do differently, and why?

The key point here is that, although the assessors might seem as if they are deeply criticising your work, they may simply be trying to get you to clarify the reasons why you have taken a certain approach. If you are clear about why you have shaped your research in the way that you have, it is simply a matter of sharing those reasons with the assessors. Therefore, it is important to have confidence in your work. While it is important to listen carefully to the questions and comments, and acknowledge the implications of the assessor's responses, there is no reason to immediately concede that your approach was not effective or to agree that you should have done something differently. This, of course, is a good preparation for negotiations in professional life.

Oral presentation

Sharing your research with your peers and tutors in an oral presentation will give you an opportunity to practise your public speaking skills, which again could seem daunting to you, but will be incredibly useful in professional life. Here, you have a chance to convince an audience of your way of thinking about your research, not only through the power of the word, but throwing the full weight of non-verbal and visual communication behind it at the same time. Therefore, in planning the presentation, consider the following:

• Do not just think about what you are going to say, but about the all-round multi-sensory experience you will be creating for your audience.
• How can you utilise the tools at your disposal to influence the audience members' thinking?
• More is not always more, and sometimes it is better to be selective and strategic about how you use those tools.

Screen-based visual aids are a great way to engage your audience visually with your material. You could show photographs or moving images of dance while you speak. If you will take time out of your presentation to show a video, keep it as brief as possible, and make sure your presentation engages with the video material in analysis or discussion. The key is not to include images as mere illustration, but use them in a way that is fundamental to or enhances the messages of your presentation. While it may be a good idea to show quotations for the audience to read while you talk, you should avoid slides that are text-heavy and duplicate the points you are saying. Instead, it is better to think about how the visual and the spoken word can complement each other, creating a multi-sensory experience for the audience.

Structure your presentation carefully, taking care to introduce and conclude your material. Try to think of ways to engage the audience with your research findings, and consider using interactive communication if appropriate. It is important to not just think about the words you are saying, but the voice's intonation and the way you hold or move your body as well.

• Will you present most effectively if you have your whole presentation scripted out?
• Or will you be more effective in your communication if you let your sentences come naturally?
• Will you be able to keep your audience engaged if you read from a page, or will you need to memorise everything?
• Or will you be somewhere in between, using a bullet point structure or flash cards?

Try to find a style that works for you and the research you are presenting.

 Focus points

• Practise your presentation a few times in advance.
• Find a willing audience of people you trust who can give you constructive feedback and boost your confidence.
• Get the timing just right.
• Omit points that are going to distract from your main message. There is nothing worse than running out of time in your presentation, and being given the signal to

stop, causing you to have to rush your final points, which are probably still very important.

- If you cannot be sure about the timing of your presentation, it is better to make it a little bit shorter, and have a few spare points that you could make or another short video that you could show at the end, if there is time.
- Practise your posture, body language, intonation and any demonstrations.

Hopefully, you will have been able to engage the audience with your material so that there are a few questions and comments at the end. Receive these graciously and gratefully, and respond to the best of your ability. However, you may also sense an underlying criticism, which is trickier to deal with in the moment. The best way to respond to criticism is to apply the guidance given in the previous section on the viva voce: reiterate your reasons for your approach and stand by them. There is no need to concede immediately. You may want to keep a brief note of each question or comment, so that you can continue to reflect on them afterwards.

 Student comments:

'What strategies were helpful for your research process?'

'When writing the piece, on occasion I met some of my peers and we discussed the work that we had done so far, including the way we had set out our work. We then assisted each other in deciding the layout that we thought would suit each other's work the most.'

'Making and sticking to regular schedules helped the process. Focusing on one section at a time also helped me.'

'Subheadings made the flow of my writing and ideas clearer.'

'When writing my dissertation, I found the online course module research information booklet and lecture presentations very useful. I developed my writing by making notes on each section, writing the text, reading it through and then changing sections as I went along. I made choices about how to present my research through looking at past dissertations and evaluating how others had set out theirs.'

Summary points:

Decide which mode of presentation you will use to present your research findings, from written text to practice-based outcomes, and negotiate this with your tutor, taking care to stay within the requirements and guidelines of your university or college.

When devising the structure of your large dissertation document, consider chapter length versus depth, as well as the notion of critical mass. Be prepared for the structure to evolve over time; a visual mapping process can help to clarify and strengthen the structure at different points in time.

Introductions, conclusions and abstracts are important sections of your dissertation text that fulfil different functions. Consider your audience carefully in writing those sections.

When constructing an argument in your dissertation text, ensure you have sufficient evidence to convince the reader of your scholarly point of view and write persuasively.

Discursive, reflective and creative writing are all commonly used in the field of dance research. Be clear about which writing style you are using when and for what purpose.

The oral communication mode used in a viva voce or presentation holds many benefits for getting your message across to your audience in a very direct way, enabling you to use non-verbal communication and visual tools. Gaining experience in speaking about your research in this way is useful for future professional situations.

Chapter 5

Beyond the dissertation, into working life

The process and benefits of the dissertation do not stop when the project is finished. Educators often aim for learning experiences to be transformative, particularly with large and extended learning opportunities such as the dissertation. Because of the transformation that is likely to come from completing such a big challenge and moving out of your comfort zone, you may carry this experience with you into later life, and indeed, into your working life.

This chapter features a number of stories from dance graduates, who have shared their experience of completing the dissertation. Engaging with their stories can yield many benefits for you, the reader. Even at the tail end of this book, you can continue to gain practical ideas about possible topics. You can also develop your understanding of how these students have approached their dissertation project to make it a success. However, perhaps most importantly, a few years after graduating, the former students reflect on the long-term benefits of the dissertation as a learning opportunity. They mention a range of transferable skills, which they were able to develop and strengthen through their dissertation research. They also describe how the dissertation challenge has influenced their personal and professional attitudes and mind-sets now that they are working in a range of areas of the dance field.

We hope that you will be inspired by these graduates' stories. As part of your reflections during the completion of your dissertation project, consider the skills you are developing for your working life, whether in or beyond the field of dance. Educational research indicates that the development of students' transferable and employability skills is strengthened if the students are explicitly aware of this skills development as part of their learning process (Rich 2015). We invite you to continue to reflect on your own dissertation experience long after graduating to continually consolidate and build on your learning.

Learning and teaching research

by Amy Guilliatt

My dissertation idea was to look into learning styles and teaching methods within practical dance classes to investigate whether there was a relationship between the two, especially to see if a student's learning style was adaptable to change to the teaching method used by the teacher. I decided to investigate this topic because I have always been interested in dance teaching, qualifying as a dance teacher at the age of 16. I wanted to use my dissertation research to improve my own abilities within teaching.

I used many research methods throughout the duration of my project. I started with using an observation process to observe the teaching methods used in practical dance classes. I then went on to determine the preferred learning style of the students who participated in my research using Kolb's Learning Style Questionnaire. I then took these results and put the students into groups depending on their learning style preference and had an interview with individual groups asking them about their thoughts about teaching methods and learning styles. After this, I brought all my data together to come up with my conclusion. I was hoping to be able to find an answer to my question, regarding dance teaching methods and learning styles, so that I could pass my research onto other dance teachers and the students. I did find there was a relationship that I could explain to teachers, enabling them to adapt their teaching style if needed.

One of the main challenges of my dissertation was at the beginning of the research project as I struggled to broaden my ideas beyond my initial research question, which was very specific. This narrow question I had chosen posed many issues regarding finding research that was already published for my literature review. I then realised that I had to take a step back to look at the wider picture of the topic I was looking into, in order to rephrase a more productive research question.

Through completing the dissertation, I developed the skill of being able to take criticism of my work and change my main idea a couple of times before I found the right one. I also developed the skill of being able to construct interview question-naires, making sure I was using questions that would get me the answers I needed for my research. I feel that this research project has strengthened my independence in being able to undertake jobs straight away without needing to ask lots of ques-tions on what I'm doing, I can now use my initiative and get on with the project.

I am currently working as a full-time dance teacher for two dance companies. My job entails teaching many different styles of dance to both adults and children, as well as the necessary administration and performance production. I aspire to be manager for one of the companies I work for in the near future, and to own my own dance school later on in my life. I still think about my dissertation project regularly, as I use different teaching methods in classes to ensure I am catering for all the different students' learning styles within the dance class.

I think the dissertation prepares students for professional life, as it is solely their own research project. They have to decide everything, from the topic to how they are going to collate the research. This helps with being independent because in the working world you aren't spoon-fed how to do things.

Practice-based choreographic project

by Anna-Lise Marie Hearn

When deciding on an idea for my dissertation, I was fascinated by the choreographic processes of William Forsythe, and in particular his 'Improvisation Technologies: A tool for the analytical dance eye', which breaks down the essential principles of his motional language. His work is acknowledged for reorienting the practice of ballet from its identification with classical repertoire to a dynamic twenty-first century art form. I was intrigued to utilise these principles that he had formalised, and use them within my own individual creative practice and the movement language that I was developing. The work that I created from this process explores the notion and complexity of manipulation of bodies and space. The opportunity for creation and manipulation is expansive and limitless. The work investigated architectural symmetry and the interplay of intellect and instinct. The dancers' roles, presence and reason for being were all challenged and explored within a complex system of structure and form. The movement derived from a combination of influences from Forsythe's technologies and my own creative technologies that I was developing and testing at the time.

In the beginning, I investigated the work of William Forsythe more deeply. I was particularly keen to utilise the methods he constructed and outlined in his 'Improvisation Technologies', so I bought myself the DVD of these, which came with a booklet detailing each process. I discovered that the video segments were originally produced by William Forsythe for the purpose of training his company's dancers, to offer them a perspective on his approach to improvisation. This was fascinating for me. … As a choreographer I realise how important it is to invest in your dancers, to develop them and grow with them, to the point where they know the way you work and move and vice versa. The fact that Forsythe had initially developed these technologies for his own dancers to understand his process better just goes to show the level of investment that you can offer your dancers to get them into a new way of moving/thinking/being. It is important to take them with you on your journey.

It was important for me to regularly rehearse my piece with my dancers. The most enriching moments and places of discovery came for me when I was in the studio with the dancers. At first it was about playing, exploring and researching these technologies. I chose to focus on a few from Forsythe and a few from my own practice that I wanted to test out. This worked very well, particularly when giving creative tasks to the dancers, as it gave a structured framework for them to explore. From this initial starting place, I continued to work collaboratively with my dancers. I would bring in a handful of ideas and creative tasks to explore in the rehearsals. From these tasks, I tended to manipulate the movement and take them further in various ways.

Once we started to structure the piece, one thing that became very important was finding the depth within the movement and the journey of the overall piece. It became about the dancers themselves. I was asking a lot of questions (of myself and the dancers); questioning the intentions within the movement, their relationships with each other, their emotional journey, their presence and what that said on stage.

I wanted to take the audience into an alternative place. I wanted them to zone into the world I had created, and become transfixed on the dancers and their powerful presence. I wanted the audience to question the dancers' intentions, presence and relationships as I had done during the creative process. I didn't want them to have it all figured out; for me that was part of the excitement. I wanted to create an experience in which each person may have their own individual emotional or physical response to the work. I aimed to create this framework, and allow space for the audience to feel, think and act on the work. I didn't want to create a narrative work that directed the audience in one straightforward journey. I wanted to communicate ideas of connection, human emotion, feeling, sensations, architecture and space… allowing room for the audience to discover these and their own connections.

One challenge I faced was to organise rehearsal times during which all of my dancers could be present. At the start, it was important for me to have all of my dancers in the studio with me for rehearsals. However, after some difficulties in organising five people's schedules and my own, and with some guidance from my tutor, I was able to rehearse effectively with those that could be there on that day. Of course this had a big influence on shaping the final piece. For example, if I only had two dancers with me in the studio one day then I was working with those two on a certain moment in the piece that perhaps the others wouldn't be in. This taught me a lot about the time and energy that goes into working with a larger number of dancers, in terms of organising rehearsal time that suits all. However, it also taught me a lot about being flexible and adaptable in situations like these and working effectively. It was a big learning experience, and one that definitely helped to prepare me for work after graduating.

Through completing the dissertation, I developed organisational skills and effective, positive ways of working with dancers and collaborators. I also developed my own choreographic voice and movement language at an early stage, using influences from other practitioners within my work. I honed my own self-motivation and the ability to motivate others and further develop the skills of the dancers I work with, seeing the potential in them and drawing that out. I learnt how to select appropriate music for the piece, working with a number of different tracks and editing it all together in a way that worked. I strengthened my ability to draw on human emotion and intention within movement to enhance a performance. I gained an understanding of the importance of effective lighting to enhance the performance, and how to work with a lighting technician during technical rehearsals to create the desired effect for the piece. Finally, I developed the ability to take constructive criticism about the work in a positive way during the creation process, particularly from peers and tutors. Don't be fearful of other people's opinions on the work. This is the reality of sharing your choreographic voice with others; it can leave you in a vulnerable position. Remember you can't please everyone; as soon as you try to do that you will lose your own voice along the way. Stay true to your initial intentions and remind yourself of these when you feel you've got a block. Go back to playing.

Using the dissertation project as an opportunity to develop my own creative practice and choreographic voice allowed me valuable time and focus, which helped me to begin to shape my work as a choreographer for the future. It strengthened my personal approach and confidence in making work, and filled me with encouragement and motivation. The response I received from the work I had created, from peers and teachers, made me feel that a door could be opening for a fulfilling and fruitful career in choreography. Another thing that shifted in me from this experience was a discovery that I felt very comfortable in a leadership role, and it led me to want to work in a creative leadership role in my professional career. I felt this would be an area in which I could personally and professionally thrive and find fulfilment and enjoyment.

I enjoyed challenging my own creative process and asking myself questions that forced me out of my comfort zone, which turned out to be an extremely valuable part of the experience as this is where you grow. The dissertation taught me about the amount of energy you need to invest, not only in rehearsals, but also in organising other peoples' schedules (your dancers, your collaborators), selecting and editing music, planning rehearsals and creative time, and any promotional work you need to do for your performance… All of these things (and more) are the reality of working within the profession, and I'm glad to have experienced that initially within a safe environment and with the support of my tutor, as it better prepared me for when I started to make my own work soon after graduating.

I now work predominantly as a freelance dance artist, choreographer/movement director and dance teacher/facilitator. I am also the artistic director of my own professional dance company, creating collaborative and eclectic works for stage, film/screen, site-specific, outdoor and non-traditional performance spaces. Alongside my choreographic work, I aim to continue to grow and develop my teaching practice. I lead and facilitate sessions for a variety of ages and abilities that sit within professional dance, vocational training for dancers, youth dance and community dance. I am also the co-director of a dance film festival, which aims to support dance film artists by providing a platform to screen, share and celebrate the work, as well as offering professional development and networking opportunities.

Not only does a practice-based dissertation give students first-hand experience in creating a work for performance, but it also allows students to experience and become aware of the other aspects involved in creating work that extend beyond the studio. It allows students to fully experience all of this in a safe environment with the support of peers, teachers and tutors. This means you can fully invest, experiment, face challenges, make mistakes and make discoveries, all within a safe framework. These early moments of creating their own work can give students an insight into that particular area of the profession, and into the role of being a choreographer. It can help shape students' decisions for when they graduate; whether they enjoy the experience and choose to pursue that direction or not – both of which are valuable.

Community dance research

by Naomi Barber

My dissertation investigated the relationship between the then current UK government (Conservative/Liberal Democrat coalition) and community dance. I investigated the government's relationship with community dance as represented in the media, focusing on two distinct community dance projects and the different approaches to working in the community they embodied. I also looked at funding cuts to the arts, investigating the historical development of arts and community dance funding in relation to the different governments the UK has had. I evaluated social hierarchies held by governments past and in 2012 and how these were reflected in arts policy.

I conducted interviews with people who worked in the community dance sector, including the directors of the community dance projects that were the focus of my research. I also reviewed published research on the topic in journals, books and websites, and participated in both community projects to gain first-hand experience. I researched arts funding and recent cuts. My dissertation argued that the government put on a display for the media to communicate the notion that they seemingly supported community dance. However, an examination of the funding cuts and what has continued to be funded reveals that in reality the government is mainly committed to supporting 'high, cultural art' rather than community arts. I read the initiation of the 'Big Dance' project, one of the case studies for my research, as a way to drum up excitement for the 2012 London Olympics. However, I argue that it was never for the community and that this is reflected in how the project operates. Nevertheless, it enables the government to look like they have an interest in supporting community dance.

The main challenges in completing my dissertation were the need to narrow down the focus of my topic and select the most relevant information from the research, before formulating this into a logical argument. I carried out substantial research outside the field of dance to help develop my knowledge and understanding of the topic in a broader sense. The hardest part was starting. I found that simply writing out my thoughts and arguments, no matter how rough to begin with, formed the starting point for my dissertation. Writing freely allowed me to clear my head, re-read my thoughts, develop, edit and grow them into the academic research project I ended up with. Re-reading and editing my work also enabled me to trim down the text and only include what was most valuable to the project. I feel I developed good time management skills, in terms of how to work through large projects in an easy and manageable way by breaking larger tasks down into smaller ones. I created a strict timetable for myself and set deadlines for each section of my work.

Undertaking the project allowed me to realise that no challenge is too large; any project is manageable if you break it down. I feel that since my dissertation I am more confident in my ability to work independently and voice my own ideas and research, and I feel motivated to work at my best and push myself. I enjoyed the independence during the research process and the ability to write about something that I was very passionate about at the time, as this gave me fuel to work hard on the topic even when I was losing the will to work. I also enjoyed the research as I gathered a lot of information about the topic, which only encouraged me to work on my dissertation and strengthen my argument.

I currently work as an administrator for a specialist dance and performing arts higher education college. My job entails supporting the smooth running of the educational programmes and providing student support. I aspire to continue to study and become a dance lecturer and continue to work in dance academia in different roles. I am about to start studying part-time for an MA in Cultural and Critical Studies in the Arts.

Although at the time many students do not see or feel it, undertaking the dissertation project helps you to develop the skills needed to adapt to new challenges and situations, which you can take with you into any area of life, particularly into your professional life. Furthermore, if you select a topic related to the field in which you wish to work, it will allow you to gain more in-depth knowledge; it never hurts to have background knowledge in your profession.

Research of cultural aspects of dance performance

by Emily Labhart

The title of my dissertation was 'White Bodies, Black Dance: The Representation of African-Caribbean Dance and Culture in the Works of Urban Bush Women'; the focus of this investigation was to outline how cultural traditions influence the dance practice of African-Caribbean forms, to then discuss whether culturally specific movement vocabularies can be performed across cultural differences, and how this potentially changes racial and cultural discourse in dance.

Using Brooklyn-based dance company Urban Bush Women as a case study, the research set out to consider how the company negotiates African-American cultural histories in its work, with particular reference to *Batty Moves* (1995), *Hands Singing Song* (1998) and *Hair Stories* (2001). It also investigated how the piece *Walking With 'Trane* (2014) and its inclusion of white female dancer Stephanie Mas presents a shift in the focus of the company, and highlights the mutability of racial identities in order to promote a more culturally inclusive dance practice. This dissertation therefore set out as an exploration of African-Caribbean dance forms in relation to the performance of cultural identity from a global perspective, to discuss the politics of changing racial representations in so-called black dance when performed by white bodies.

There were limitations to the research in terms of not being able to observe live performances of the company and the works in question due to it being based in Brooklyn, USA. This meant the investigation relied heavily on film footage, photographs and reviews of the company in order to analyse movement and choreography. The dissertation utilised theories such as postcolonialism, hybridity and cultural representation through the works of Fanon, Gilroy, Bhabha and DeFrantz. The aim was to reaffirm that identity is socially constructed rather than fixed, and that these notions are entangled with colonial discourse considering key historical markers such as the Transatlantic Slave Trade and the Civil Rights Movement.

'White Bodies, Black Dance' explores how the choreographic voice/identity of Urban Bush Women underwent change by the addition of Mas and the wider context in which this journey took place. The argument outlined two opposing views of hybridity and globalisation before considering DeFrantz's notion of 'post-race performance', where companies seek to avoid racial profiles that circumscribe their work as a creative strategy for unalienated modes of expression. Through this research, I came to the conclusion that Jawole Willa Jo Zollar is attempting to move past a space of exclusivity that has defined her work since the company's inception in 1984, to allow the company to build a more inclusive dance community where racial determinations become less significant. This is important for the global development of dance practices, where frontiers of racial identity can become blurred in order to displace previous notions of power and privilege, providing a greater scope of creativity beyond the colour line.

The 12,000 word dissertation is the largest piece of research I have undertaken so far and it facilitated the development of a number of skills, namely: time-management, how to structure a cohesive argument, independent study, writing sensitively about difficult topics and being able to work with a range of sources effectively. A challenge for me when writing the dissertation was deciding what parts of my research to include and what to omit. It can feel almost wasteful to accumulate research and not include it in the final write-up, but it will always inform your argument and make you more knowledgeable in your subject area – which will undoubtedly come across in your dissertation.

These skills have translated into my current role as Access and Education Projects Co-ordinator for a middle-scale contemporary dance repertory company, where I am responsible for managing a variety of projects including work in the areas of widening participation, the hard to reach, cross-curricular collaboration, arts award, partnership coordination and youth dance events, as well as writing funding applications and evaluative reports. The dissertation prepares students for professional working contexts by demonstrating commitment, encouraging critical thinking, formulating a balanced argument and building confidence in developing ideas and opinions in order to plan and deliver work effectively. I discussed my dissertation in my interview for my current role, as the dance company I work for has perhaps followed a similar trajectory in terms of choreographic identity. It was a good opportunity for open conversation and I would like to think that this contextual awareness contributed to my success in the post.

The writing of 'White Bodies, Black Dance' (and my studies leading up to it) have encouraged my aspirations to undertake MA research in the areas of post-colonialism and global policy, with the hopes to becoming an arts manager before going on to become a lecturer/researcher within the field.

My advice for students about to begin their undergraduate dissertation is to:

1. Choose a topic that you are genuinely interested in. You will be spending a significant amount of time on researching and writing this piece of work so it should be something you care about.
2. Always do some light research on a few topics before making a final decision. There is no point making the process more challenging for yourself by selecting a topic or area of thinking that doesn't have much research already in existence. This is where the literature review comes in. As an undergraduate, you won't be making revolutionary discoveries in your dissertation (this only comes at PhD level), therefore choose a subject area that has some critical thinking in publication already that you can feed from. Your work will still be valuable, but it will also be well supported.
3. Select a research question/topic that is bigger than dance. By this, I mean to choose theoretical lenses or modes of thinking that are applicable to a range of discourses (whether within the arts, society as a whole or on a global scale), as this will make your argument transferable to a range of contexts and will give you a more rounded world-view.

The dissertation should inspire you, allow you to learn new things and develop your thinking. It will be a huge part of your final year and can help guide your future career choices. I really enjoyed writing my dissertation and look forward to researching and thinking critically again in future study. Enjoy the journey, give yourself plenty of time and make it count.

Finally...

The above stories are examples of former students who have reflected on their learning experience and responded to their tutors' advice about the relevance of the dissertation as a learning opportunity for their professional lives. At the very end of this book, we want to encourage you to stay in touch with the tutors at your institution and share with them what the dissertation has meant for you, once you have had a chance to see how it has impacted on your career.

Activity: One or more years after graduating...

Take a moment to remember your dissertation project. Perhaps re-read it or look again at your dissertation project materials. Make a note of the sense of this reflection.

What are you proud of?

Was there anything you had forgotten was there?

Did anything surprise you at the time?

Would you have added anything or taken a different direction?

What did you do after your dissertation and upon graduating?

Can you identify the skills and attributes that you developed through the research?

How are these employed in your current activities?

Share these reflections with your former tutor, and with us, if you would like. Your insights may be useful to future students.

 Student comments:

'Did your research influence your future plans?'

'My topic choice was directly linked to the field that I wanted to move into. Initially, it assisted me on getting onto an MSc in Sport and Exercise Physiology. My dissertation project had to be directly linked to dance instead of fitness in general, so I chose to look at aerobic fitness in dancers and injuries. This was because in the future I wanted to potentially start a PhD. My future research interest is exertion and how the body can face extreme situations, such as with astronauts, deep-sea divers, mountaineers, etc. Therefore, by starting to look at the ways in which fatigue affects dancers, I was able to start to see how the body reacts to fatigue and how it can be affected by changes in the environment.'

'I chose to do my dissertation on teaching and learning in different styles of dance, because I have taught from the age of 16 and it was something I was interested in. When I left university I wanted to perform. At the moment I am teaching full time, so my dissertation has influenced my career choices.'

'The process of working on writing for a year provided me with organisational skills. Through encouragement from my supervisor I developed determination and discipline to carry my work through to the finish. In the future I hope to teach dance; therefore, basing my dissertation on learning processes in dance became the main focus of my writing.'

Summary points:

Completing your dissertation project enables you to further develop the transferable skills and personal and professional attitudes needed for future employment.

The stories from the four dance graduates connect their dissertation experience to their current careers in various parts of the field.

We want to encourage you to continue to reflect on the dissertation learning experience after you graduate. Stay in touch with your tutors and share with them how the dissertation has helped to prepare you for professional life.

References

Adshead, J. (ed.) (1988) *Dance Analysis: Theory and Practice*. London: Dance Books.

Adshead-Lansdale, J. and Layson, J. (eds.) (1994) *Dance History: An Introduction*. 2nd edn, London: Routledge.

Amans, D. (ed.) (2008) *An Introduction to Community Dance Practice*. Basingstoke: Palgrave Macmillan.

Berg, K.E. and Latin, R.W. (2008) *Essentials of Research Methods in Health, Physical Education, Exercise Science, and Recreation*. 3rd edn, Baltimore, MD: Lippincott Williams & Wilkins.

Blanco Borelli, M. (ed.) (2014) *The Oxford Handbook of Dance and the Popular Screen*. Oxford: Oxford University Press.

Broadhurst, S. and Machon, J. (eds.) (2006) *Performance and Technology: Practices of Virtual Embodiment and Interactivity*. Basingstoke: Palgrave Macmillan.

Buckland, T.J. (1999) *Dance in the Field: Theory, Methods and Issues in Dance Ethnography*. Basingstoke: Palgrave Macmillan.

Burrows, J. (2010) *A Choreographer's Handbook*. Abingdon, Oxon: Routledge.

Butterworth, J. and Wildschut, L. (eds.) (2009) *Contemporary Choreography: A Critical Reader*. London: Routledge.

Carter, A. (ed.) (2004) *Rethinking Dance History: A Reader*. London: Routledge.

Cooper, S. (2007) *Staging Dance*. London: Routledge.

Cooper Albright, A. (1997) *Choreographing Difference: The Body and Identity in Contemporary Dance*. Hanover, NH: Wesleyan University Press.

Counsell, C. and Wolf, L. (eds.) (2001) *Performance Analysis: An Introductory Coursebook*. London: Routledge.

Dankworth, L.E. and David, A.R. (eds.) (2014) *Dance Ethnography and Global Perspectives: Identity, Embodiment and Culture*. Basingstoke: Palgrave Macmillan.

Davida, D. (2011) *Fields in Motion: Ethnography in the Worlds of Dance*. Ontario: Wilfrid Laurier University Press.

Descartes, R. (1644). *Principia Philosophiae*.

Dils, A. and Cooper Albright, A. (eds.) (2001) *Moving History/Dancing Cultures: A Dance History Reader*. Middletown, CT: Wesleyan University Press.

Dixon, S. (2007) *Digital Performance: A History of New Media in Theater, Dance, Performance Art, and Installation*. Cambridge, MA: MIT Press.

Dodds, S. (2001) *Dance on Screen: Genres and Media from Hollywood to Experimental Art*. Basingstoke: Palgrave Macmillan.

Dodds, S. (2011) *Dancing on the Canon: Embodiments of Value in Popular Dance*. Basingstoke: Palgrave Macmillan.

Foster, S.L. (1986) *Reading Dancing: Bodies and Subjects in Contemporary American Dance*. Berkeley, CA: University of California Press.

(ed.) (1996) *Corporealities: Dancing Knowledge, Culture and Power*. London: Routledge.

Gibbons, E. (2007) *Teaching Dance: The Spectrum of Styles*. Bloomington, IN: AuthorHouse.

Govan, E., Nicholson, H. and Ormington, K. (2007) *Making a Performance: Devising Histories and Contemporary Practices*. London: Routledge.

Grau, A. and Jordan, S. (eds.) (2000) *Europe Dancing: Perspectives on Theatre, Dance, and Cultural Identity*. London: Routledge.

Green, D.F. (2010) *Choreographing From Within: Developing the Habit of Inquiry as an Artist*. Champaign, IL: Human Kinetics.

Hamera, J. (2006) *Dancing Communities: Performance, Difference and Connection in the Global City*. Basingstoke: Palgrave Macmillan.

Hopgood, J. (2016) *Dance Production: Design and Technology*. New York: Focal Press.

Howard, P. (2002) *What is Scenography?* London: Routledge.

Jasper, L. and Siddall, J. (1999) *Managing Dance: Current Issues and Future Strategies*. Horndon: Northcote House.

Jones, E.L. and Ryan, M.E. (2015) The Dancer as Reflective Practitioner. In: Ryan, Mary Elizabeth (ed.) *Teaching Reflective Learning in Higher Education: A Systematic Approach Using Pedagogic Patterns*. Berlin: Springer International Publishing, pp. 51–64.

Kassing, G. (2007) *History of Dance: An Interactive Arts Approach*. Champaign, IL: Human Kinetics.

Kassing G. and Jay D.M. (2003) *Dance Teaching Methods and Curriculum Design: Comprehensive K-12 Dance Education*. Champaign, IL: Human Kinetics.

Kolb, D.A. (2014) *Experiential Learning: Experience as the Source of Learning and Development*. 2nd edn, New Jersey: Pearson FT Press.

Kozel, S. (2007) *Closer: Performance, Technologies, Phenomenology*. Cambridge, MA: MIT Press.

Kumar, R. (2014) *Research Methodology: A Step-by-Step Guide for Beginners*. 4th edn, London: SAGE Publications.

Kuppers, P. (2007) *Community Performance: An Introduction*. London: Routledge.

McPherson, K. (2006) *Making Video Dance*. London: Routledge.

Midgelow, V.L. and Bacon, J.M. (eds.) *Choreographic Practices* journal, first published in 2010 and electronically available.

Minton, S.C. (2007) *Choreography: A Basic Approach Using Improvisation*. 3rd edn, Champaign, IL: Human Kinetics.

Newlove, J. and Dalby, J. (2004) *Laban for All*. New York, NY: Routledge.

Padgett, A.D. (2010) *How to Set Up a Successful Dance Class in 6 Easy Steps*. Dancing Detectives.

Payne, H.L. (2006) *Dance Movement Therapy Theory: Research and Practice*. 2nd edn, London: Routledge.

Preston-Dunlop, V. (1998) *Looking at Dances: A Choreological Perspective on Choreography*. London: Verve Publishing.

Preston-Dunlop, V. and Sanchez-Colberg, A. (2002) *Dance and the Performative*. London: Verve.

Pugh McCutchen, B. (2006) *Teaching Dance as Art in Education*. Champaign, IL: Human Kinetics.

Quin, E., Rafferty, S. and Tomlinson, C. (2015) *Safe Dance Practice: An Applied Dance Science Perspective*. Champaign, IL: Human Kinetics.

Reynolds, D. and Reason, M. (2012) *Kinesthetic Empathy in Creative and Cultural Practices*. Bristol: Intellect.

Rich, J. (2015) *Employability: Degrees of Value*. Occasional Paper 12. Higher Education Policy Institute.

Savyasaachi (1998) Unlearning Fieldwork: The Flight of an Arctic Tern. In: Thapan, M. (ed.) *Anthropological Journeys: Reflections on Fieldwork*. New Delhi: Orient Longman, pp. 83–113.

Smith-Autard, J.M. (2002) *The Art of Dance in Education*. London: A&C Black Publishers.

Sörgel, S. (2015) *Dance and the Body in Western Theatre: 1948 to the Present*. Basingstoke: Palgrave Macmillan.

Thomas, H. (2003) *The Body, Dance and Cultural Theory*. Basingstoke: Palgrave Macmillan.

Whatley, S., Garrett Brown, N. and Alexander, K. (2015) *Attending to Movement: Somatic Perspectives on Living in This World*. Axminster: Triarchy Press.

Index